BRIAN TRACY'S
MASTER  COURSE FOR
BUSINESS
SUCCESS

BRIAN TRACY'S

MASTER

COURSE FOR

BUSINESS

SUCCESS

MEDIA

Published 2024 by Gildan Media LLC
aka G&D Media
www.GandDmedia.com

Cover design by Tom McKeveny

Interior design by Meghan Day Healey of Story Horse, LLC

Library of Congress Cataloging-in-Publication Data is available upon request

ISBN: 978-1-7225-0672-8

10   9   8   7   6   5   4   3   2   1

Contents

Twelve Master Skills for Success 7

Preface 9

1 The Fine Art of Communication 11

2 Everything Is Negotiable 43

3 Why You Should Start Your Own Business 75

4 How to Get Startup Capital 117

5 Get Your Message Across 139

6 Your Financial Future in Real Estate 165

7 The How and Why of Money—Yours and Other People's 207

Twelve Master Skills
for Success

1. Maximize your potential.
2. Understand the mental laws of the universe.
3. Employ strategic thinking.
4. Set meaningful and powerful goals.
5. Use the Twelve-Step process to revolutionize your life.
6. Tap into the power of the superconscious mind.
7. Master time management.
8. Streamline your life.
9. Increase your earning ability.
10. Find the career that you really want.
11. Use the power of leverage.
12. Achieve financial independence.

Preface

The principles that you are about to read have been proven and tested for decades, if not centuries, by some of the most successful people who have ever lived.

As you will see, they are not necessarily difficult to understand, although their execution requires constant effort and attention. Few people are willing to put in this effort. That's why few people are successful.

The first two chapters of this book describe two of the most important skills you could possibly develop: communication and negotiation. Your ability to communicate clearly with others—and that means understanding them as well as making yourself understood—is vital not only to your happiness but to your survival. Your capacity to negotiate—to ask for what you want and to get it—is equally important in all areas of life.

The following chapters focus more specifically on the skills and qualities needed for entrepreneurial success, that is, the ability to create and profit from a business. As you'll learn, practically everyone can accomplish this. It just requires the mastery of certain skills and principles that you'll explore in detail here, including getting the capital you need to start out and leveraging the skills of others to profit, while enabling them to profit as well.

You'll also learn in detail how business is ultimately a matter of selling: convincing other people that your product or service is desirable and will solve some problem or satisfy some desire of theirs. You'll learn the finer points of selling, not only in person but through advertising and publicity.

Finally, you will learn on a step-by-step basis how to achieve financial success through real estate, even if you have no money to start out with. You'll learn how to leverage OPM—other people's money—and, starting small, build a real estate empire.

No matter what your situation or your ambitions may be, the knowledge that you'll acquire in these pages will show you the way to greater happiness and success in your work and every other area of your life. You are now embarking on an exciting and profitable adventure.

1

The Fine Art of Communication

Your ability to communicate is perhaps the most important single skill that you can develop. Fully 85 percent of your success in your work and personal life will come from your ability to communicate and interact effectively with other people.

There are two forms of communication: interpersonal and intrapersonal. Interpersonal communication includes all of your interactions with other people. Intrapersonal communications are those with yourself. You can immediately do a great number of things to improve the quality of your communications. You begin by going to work on yourself. All human interaction is from the inside out. You communicate what you are, and what you are is largely determined by your belief systems, by your self-concept.

You communicate what you are.

The Importance of Self-Image

What's going on in your own mind is the most important single determinant of your interpersonal communications. The law of expression says that whatever is *impressed* will be *expressed*. Your self-concept is the totality of your beliefs and ideas about yourself, formed as the result of every impression, decision, choice, and action that you've taken since you were an infant. As an adult, you do not believe what you see, but rather you *see* what you *believe*. Put another way, what you *see* is what you *are*. Every event in the world around you, including and especially your human interactions, is colored and shaded by your personality. The way you talk, walk, behave, and experience other people is determined more by your own mental programming than by any other factor.

Your self-image, how you see yourself and think about yourself, is made up of three elements: (1) the way you see yourself; (2) the way that others see you; and (3) the way you think others see you.

Your self-esteem involves how much you like and respect yourself: how much you feel yourself to be a valuable and worthwhile person. When you experience high self-esteem, you tend to have an integrated self-image: the way you see yourself, the way you think others see you, and the way they actually do see you will be the same. There will be little or no conflict or disagreement in your various images of yourself, and therefore there will be little conflict or disagreement between yourself and others.

Another element of your intrapersonal communications is how good you feel you are at what you do. This is called *self-efficacy* or *performance-based self-esteem*.

When you like and respect yourself and you know you're good at what you do, you tend to enjoy a positive self-image that is immediately recognizable to other people. As you develop and improve internally, the quality of your relationships with others will improve automatically and effortlessly.

For this reason, your ongoing inner dialogue will have more of an impact on the quality of your communications than any other factor. The law of expectation says that whatever you expect with confidence tends to become your own self-fulfilling prophecy. Dr. Robert Rosenthal of Harvard demonstrated repeatedly that your expectations have a powerful impact on your outcomes. When teachers or parents expect young people to do well, they tend to do far better than they would in the absence of those expectations. When friends, bosses, or other people we respect tell us they believe we are capable of doing certain things successfully, their confidence often overcomes our own skepticism and causes us to do better than we otherwise would.

Whatever you expect tends to become your own self-fulfilling prophecy.

Similarly, your own expectations about yourself and your abilities have an enormous impact on how you behave and how people react to you. One of the most identifiable signs of a winning human being is an ongoing attitude of confident self-expectancy: expecting things to turn out well in advance. It means continually looking for the good in people and situations. Whenever you meet a new person expecting the other person to like you and expecting to like the other person, the probability of both occurring goes up dramatically. If you expect to be successful, liked, and popular, to be listened to, and to enjoy your relationships with others, you will seldom be disappointed.

Positive affirmations can be helpful in programming your mind for success. You can say things like, "I can hardly wait for this meeting," or, "I know everything is going to turn out well." When you repeat these affirmations to yourself with enthusiasm and conviction, your subconscious mind goes to work to make your actions and reactions consistent with these dominant thoughts. You can use this quick affirmation technique prior to a date, a sales call, an important interview, or even a public talk. It works virtually every single time.

Creative Visualization

Another exercise for improving your intrapersonal communications, the quality of your personality, and the messages you give yourself is creative visualization. The inner mirror or mental picture that you carry around of yourself is the key determinant of your effectiveness with others.

You can improve your self-image by repeatedly projecting on the screen of your mind a picture of yourself performing at your best. When you visualize and emotionalize an exciting picture of a successful event, real or imagined, your subconscious mind accepts this picture as a command, as operating instructions. It then goes to work to modify your self-confidence, enthusiasm, body language, tone of voice, and facial expression. This kind of visualization, repeated over and over again, eventually locks in and becomes a natural and spontaneous part of your personality. You develop the habit of a positive mental attitude.

Everyone starts off in life with an inferiority complex. For the first few years of our lives, we see ourselves as small, defenseless, and vulnerable. If we've also been subjected to destructive criticism by our parents during these years, we will tend to grow up feeling that we are not as good as other people. Yet most successful and popular men and women also grow up with feelings of inferiority, but overcame them as the result of long, hard work. Your self-concept and your personality are not easily changed, but they can definitely be improved if you set it as a goal and go to work on it.

When I was growing up, I was terribly unpopular. As a child and teenager, I spent much of my time alone. I got into trouble in school, and neither teachers nor other students wanted to have anything to do with me. I was never invited to parties, and virtually no girl wanted to be seen with me. In an attempt to be liked, I seemed to do and say all the wrong things. I shot off my mouth in class. I interrupted with smart-aleck remarks and behaved in such a way that I ended up with very few friends. It took me many years of working on myself to understand how my personality had developed this way and to learn how to change.

Perhaps the most important thing that happened to me was learning how to set goals and achieve them. As I developed a sense of my own worth based on accomplishment, I began to like and respect myself more, and pretty soon other people began to like me as well. You can develop a positive, powerful, and pleasing personality that will enable you to enjoy the success, happiness, and pleasure that comes from happy relationships by setting it as a goal and working on yourself continually every single day.

Virtually everything we get comes as a result of interacting effectively with others.

Interpersonal Communication

Virtually everything we get comes as a result of interacting effectively with others. Skilled communicators rise to the top of every field and occupation. Your ability to get your point across in such a way that others want to help you is central to everything you might want to achieve.

The best communication tool is a positive mental attitude.

Perhaps the best communication tool is a positive mental attitude. The habit of keeping your conversation generally positive and optimistic will cause you to be liked and accepted in more places and by more people than any other single factor. Cheerfulness arising from a positive self-image and a deep sense of your own value will surround you like a warm light, triggering positive responses in everyone you meet. In study after study, the most effective and respected people have been described with the word *nice*. When you are regarded as a nice person, all kinds of doors will open for you, and people will be eager to help and cooperate with you.

In psychology, this type of behavior is called *unconditional positive regard*: remaining positive and supportive no matter what the other person says. Psychotherapists know that the key to helping clients work through their problems is to create a relationship where the client feels safe and secure. Only when a troubled person feels completely accepted can they verbalize and work through the problem. If the client is angry or upset, the psychotherapist responds with support and empathy. If the client criticizes or condemns some other person or situation, the psychotherapist refuses to be caught up in the negative emotions, merely nodding and smiling, allowing and encouraging the other person to fully vent their feelings. See yourself as a psychotherapist or a good friend to yourself.

Many people are poor communicators because their egos are so involved in the interaction that they become unaware of the other person. They are so concerned about themselves that they use others merely as sounding boards. They're not really interested in hearing about the other person's situation; they're merely seeking an opportunity to express their own feelings and opinions.

As you develop self-esteem and self-acceptance, you become less preoccupied with yourself and more interested in others.

Fortunately, as you develop higher levels of self-esteem and self-acceptance, you naturally become less preoccupied with yourself and more interested in others. One way to accelerate this development is by acting the part: pretending to find the other person completely fascinating. If you pretend to find another person interesting for any period of time, they will open up to you and reveal to you facts about themselves that you will actually find fascinating. In less than five minutes of pretending interest in another person, you'll be engrossed in what that person has to share with you. This is a real secret of excellent human relations. The life of virtually everyone you will ever meet will turn out to be fascinating if you give them an opportunity to tell you about it. When you get your ego out of the way and allow the other person's ego to express itself, you'll quickly become an excellent communicator.

Misunderstandings and Noise

The president of a large company told me recently that 99 percent of the problems in his organization stem from poor or incomplete

communication. In my consulting work with hundreds of corporations, I've never found a company in which the executives and staff
did not feel that communications could be improved. This is probably true for most families and relationships as well.

When we examine the actual process of communication, it's
easy to see why misunderstandings arise. If you want to communicate with another person, you conceive of the idea that you wish to
convey and you encode it in words, which you send in the form of a
message. This message may be spoken face-to-face, by telephone, or
in a written form. The other person must decode or translate your
message to get the meaning that you're trying to convey.

Similarly, the recipient conceives of a reply in the form of a
thought, encodes it in words, and sends the message to you; you in
turn receive and decode that message. This process takes place even
in the simplest conversations. What could be simpler?

Many factors can cause possible distortion of the message. We
call these factors *noise*—like the noise or interference that you sometimes hear on a telephone line or when you're tuning into a radio
station. There are several kinds of noise. *Physical noise* refers to factors in the physical environment such as cigarette smoke, radio or
television, traffic, children screaming, an airplane flying over, a car
going past, or any other factor that might interfere with the clear
reception of a message. If you're surrounded by noise, if you're tired
or uncomfortable, or if the room is too hot or too cold, it becomes
hard to concentrate on what the other person is saying.

Then there's *physiological noise*. This refers to what is going on
inside the person during the communication. The person may be
suffering from fatigue or illness, may have a sore tooth or be preoccupied with some problem. The person may be angry or defensive
about the message. They may also either like or dislike you, respect

or not respect you, might find what you are saying interesting or not interesting. Imagine trying to communicate with someone with a toothache who has just had an argument with her boss and is not particularly interested in the subject. Do you see how easy it would be for the communication to break down?

There are also the differences between verbal and nonverbal meanings. Dr. Albert Mehrabian, a specialist in communications, has determined that only 7 percent of the message that we send is contained in the words themselves: 38 percent is contained in the tone of voice, and 55 percent is contained in the body language and in the nonverbal gestures that accompany the message. We are very sensitive to both verbal and nonverbal cues, and if the body language and tone of voice contradict the words, we tend to disbelieve the words. In a telephone conversation, the tone of voice becomes perhaps 85 percent of the message. When the only message is what you hear through the phone, even a pause or hesitation becomes an important part of the communication.

In addition to these factors, there's the issue of the meaning of words. Sometimes the right or wrong choice of words can have critical and far-reaching consequences. In the English language, there are a total of 470,000 words, according to Merriam-Webster's Dictionary. There are also more than 14,000 meanings for the 500 most common words that we use in our day-to-day lives. Is it any wonder that there are so many misunderstandings?

It's been said that God gave us two ears and one mouth and that we should use them in the same proportions: we should listen twice as much as we speak. Herein lies the key to being a good communicator. To ensure that the message that you send is the one that is received and the message that you receive is the one intended, you need to do two things. First, you need to accept 100 percent responsibility not only for being understood but also for understanding. Stephen Covey recommends that you seek first to understand and only then to be understood. Most of us are so eager to get other people to understand us that we overlook the importance of understanding them. When you seek first to understand the other person, you're much more likely to communicate the right words in the right way and create a desire in them to understand you as well.

Seek first to understand, and only then to be understood.

Second, to be a good communicator, you need to learn to be more sensitive, not only to the words but to the meanings that the other person attaches to the words. You need to be aware of both verbal and nonverbal messages. Listen with your whole mind to be sure that what you are hearing and what they're saying are the same.

Forms of Nonlistening

The best communicators are not necessarily great talkers, but they are excellent listeners. It's been estimated that managers, executives, and leaders spend as much as 50 percent of their time listening to other people, but most people are poor listeners or what we might call nonlisteners. They make the mistake of thinking that they are listening, when in reality they're merely going through one or more exercises in nonlistening.

Because nonlistening is the major reason for misunderstandings and miscommunications, it's important to be aware of the various forms of nonlistening to make sure you are not guilty of any of them.

The first form of nonlistening is *pseudolistening* or phony listening. Pseudolistening is an imitation of the real thing. The pseudolistener gives the appearance of being attentive. He looks you in the eye, nods and smiles at the right times, and may even answer you occasionally, but behind that appearance of interest, something entirely different is going on. Pseudolisteners use a polite facade to mask thoughts that have nothing to do with what the speaker is saying. Often the pseudolistener is ignoring you because something on his or her mind is more important than what you are saying. Pseudolisteners may be bored or think they have already heard what you have to say before, so they tune out your remarks. Whatever the reasons, pseudolistening is really counterfeit communication, and that soon becomes obvious to the other party.

The second form of non-listening is *stage hogging*. The stage hog is only interested in expressing their own ideas and doesn't care about what anyone else has to say. The stage hog will allow you to speak from time to time, but only so that they can catch their breath and use your remarks as a reason to go on babbling (or keep you from running away). Stage hogs don't really hold conversations; they're really making a speech and using the opportunity to dominate others with their talk.

The third form of nonlistening is *selective listening*. Selective listeners respond only to the parts of your remarks that interest them and reject everything else. Unless you're talking about something that specifically interests them, they simply tune you out and think of other things. Selective listening is a form of selfish listening in that the listener is concerned only about himself or herself.

Another form of nonlistening is *insulated listening*. Insulated listeners avoid topics they would rather not talk about. They simply fail to hear or acknowledge them. If you remind them of a problem or bring something up they don't want to deal with, they will nod, answer you, and promptly ignore what you just said.

Defensive listening is a form of nonlistening in which the listener takes things that you intended as innocent comments and turns them into personal attacks. A person with a poor self-image or low self-esteem often reads into the most casual remarks a criticism or comment on their behavior and reacts defensively by striking back. This is especially true with hypersensitive men and women—those who have been subjected to a lot of destructive criticism during their formative years.

Yet another form of nonlistening is *ambushing*. The typical ambusher is a person who listens to what you're saying while seeking for an opportunity to attack or disagree with you. The ambusher looks for differences between what you're saying and his or her point of view. When the ambusher picks up even a small piece of conflicting data in your conversation, he or she immediately uses it to counterattack.

The final form is *insensitive listening*. Insensitive listeners make no effort to understand what the other person is really trying to say. They take the words of the other person at face value and make no effort to interpret the feelings behind the words. This kind of insensitivity unfortunately often occurs between men and women in relationships.

Almost everyone is guilty of being a nonlistener or a poor listener from time to time. If your goal is to become an excellent communicator, it's important to be aware of the reasons for the tendencies and temptations not to listen and to pay full attention to people when they're speaking to you.

Why We Don't Listen

One reason we don't listen as well as we could is message overload. You probably spend half of the time you're awake taking in verbal messages from bosses, friends, coworkers, family, salespeople, and others. You are bombarded with commercial messages from the Internet, radio, television, magazines and newspapers. Because of this overload, you often let your attention wander just to give yourself a break.

Preoccupation is another reason you don't always listen carefully. Often you get so wrapped up in your own personal concerns that it's hard to pay attention to someone else. Instead, you go through the motions of pseudolistening, nodding, smiling, and pretending that you're paying attention when in reality your mind is miles away.

Another reason for poor listening is the fact that there's a difference in the number of words you can understand and the number of words that another person can speak. Your mind can understand speech at a rate of 600 words per minute, whereas the average person speaks at a rate of 125 to 150 words per minute. This means you have fully three quarters of the time when another person is speaking to think of other things. Your attention can wander to other subjects while you still appear to be listening and in fact probably are still taking in most of what the other person is saying. It takes tremendous self-discipline to control your attention and concentrate on the various levels of meaning contained in the words the other person is speaking, but the payoff in higher-quality communications makes it worth the effort.

We often don't listen well because we feel that talking has more advantages than listening.

We often don't listen well because we feel that talking has more advantages than listening. It seems to us that we have more to gain by speaking because it gives us a chance to control the thoughts and actions of the other person. Often we feel that it gives us the chance to gain the admiration, respect, or liking of others. If we tell jokes or offer advice or tell them all we know about a particular subject, they will like us or be impressed by us. If we instead stand quietly and say very little, they may think that we have nothing worthwhile to say. Also, talking gives you a chance to release energy in a way that listening can't. We get a lot of pleasure out of expressing ourselves to others and talking about things that interest or concern us personally. Unfortunately, it can get to the point where we fall in love with the sound of our own voice and go on talking without concern for the conversational needs of others.

Finally, we often don't listen well because we're not trained to do it. A common mistake is to think that listening is like breathing: you do it naturally because you're alive. The truth is that listening is a skill, very much like speaking: although everybody does it, very few do it well. Learning to listen well can do more to help your relationships and your career than perhaps any other single quality that you can develop.

**People don't care how much you know
until they know how much you care.**

Friendship and Empathy

There's an old saying that people don't care how much you know until they know how much you care. The key to good listening is the friendship factor: the fact that people want and need to be liked and will not allow themselves to be influenced by someone until they're convinced that that person is their friend.

The friendship factor is built on the three Cs: *caring, courtesy*, and *consideration*. The best communicators tend to be sensitive to others and project an attitude of caring about the thoughts and concerns of the other person. Everyone needs to feel valued by others, and the instant this connection takes place between two people, good communications begin to flow naturally. You can remember many experiences where you've met a person and had an instant feeling of rapport. You were able to talk naturally and spontaneously for a long time on a variety of subjects with pleasure and satisfaction.

Good communicators create this kind of experience with far more people far faster and more easily. This happens when you put aside your preoccupation with yourself and focus your attention onto the other person. Perhaps the best method for building and maintaining high-quality relationships is empathetic listening, or listening to help. There's a saying that everyone you meet is carrying a heavy load. In this form of listening, you encourage people to talk about their problems and concerns, and then you help them to work their problems out for themselves. Often what a person needs more than anything else is just a good sounding board. Someone who will listen and give proper responses can help the person come to his or her own conclusions. Indeed much of modern psychotherapy is based on the idea that the patient is capable of self-healing if the proper listening relationship is established.

Empathetic listening is probably the best method for building and maintaining high-quality relationships.

The Problem with Advice

When someone discusses a problem, the first and most natural tendency is to give advice. It's been well said that the propensity to give advice is universal—but don't worry, because the propensity to ignore advice is also universal. People seldom take advice, no matter how good or well-intentioned it is. Often people don't want advice at all. They merely want an opportunity to talk out the problem with someone they trust before resolving it themselves.

If you are going to offer advice, you need to be sure that three conditions are present:

1. Be confident that your advice is correct. Just because a course of action worked for you doesn't mean it will work for someone else.

2. Be sure the person seeking your advice is truly ready to accept it. Sometimes the person will seemingly ask your advice while intending to do something else anyway.

3. Make sure that the other person won't blame you if the advice doesn't work out. You must make it clear that although you may be offering suggestions, the choice and responsibility of following them are up to the other person.

Action Exercise

Here is an action exercise for you: Select one person—the most important person in your life—and practice being a good listener with that person. Train yourself to be aware of their words and the feelings behind the words. See if you can develop a deeper understanding of how and why the person feels the way they do. In addition, observe the interactions of others, including the quality of communication (or lack of it). Notice the problems that arise when people do not communicate clearly or listen attentively. Above all, work on your own ability to communicate with your spouse, your children, your boss, your coworkers, and your friends. See what a difference this will make in your relationships and the quality of everything you do.

Four Personality Types

If you study how people think and respond, you can dramatically increase the likelihood of persuading them to do what you want. A tremendous amount of research has been done on personality styles and different ways of thinking and responding. Researchers have determined that there are two scales of behavior, which divide personalities into four basic types.

FOUR PERSONALITY TYPES

	People-Oriented	Task-Oriented
Introvert	Amiable	Thinker
Extravert	Expressive	Driver

The first scale of behavior is *introvert* versus *extravert*. Introverted people are quiet and inward-thinking in their interactions and behavior. Extraverts are expressive and outgoing with their thoughts and feelings.

The second scale is *people orientation* versus *task orientation*. A person who is people-oriented thinks of people as the central focus of his or her life and activities. Task-oriented people are more concerned with getting the job done than with the impact of their behavior on others.

When you combine these two grids, you get the four basic styles: the *relator* or *amiable* personality; the *analytical* or the *thinker personality*; the *driver* or *director*; and the *expressive* or *socializer* personality.

The *amiable* or *relator* personality is introverted or indirect in their manner of expression but is also intensely people-oriented. These individuals tend to be very concerned with feelings. They are sensitive, and their primary motivation is to get along well with others. Amiables are attracted toward fields such as the helping professions—teachers, nurses, psychologists, guidance counselors, and social workers—where they can talk to and relate personally with others on a one-to-one basis.

If you're trying to sell an idea to an amiable, you would point out how it would positively benefit relationships among people, how it would enable them to be happier, feel better, and get along better. Amiables place a high value on teamwork and acceptance.

If you were selling a house to an amiable, you would point out how beautifully the house is designed for socializing. You would suggest how the family would be able to get together in this room, the children would play happily with this layout, and that friends and relatives would be impressed with the design and structure of the home, but you would be low-pressure and low-key. The amiable makes decisions slowly and only after plenty of thought.

The second type of personality is the *thinker* or the *analytic*. This person is indirect, task-oriented, and concerned with details. Thinkers are neither people-oriented nor extraverted but take great pride in doing things well: they are fastidious about accuracy and neatness. The thinker or analytical personality style is mostly found in accounting, bookkeeping, engineering, administration, computer programming, and other fields that require careful attention to detail.

When you deal with a thinker, they will always ask you a lot of penetrating and detail-oriented questions. The best way to persuade this type of person is to answer these questions fully and with exact facts and figures. If you were selling to an analytical personality, they would ask a lot of questions about technical and performance specifications, price terms, and small details. With this type of person, you should focus on being low-keyed and very accurate with your facts.

The third personality style is the *driver* or *director*. The driver is both extraverted and intensely task-oriented. This person is most concerned with results, with getting the job done efficiently, effectively, and at the lowest possible cost. The driver has a low level (and sometimes no level) of concern for the people involved. You'll find drivers in fields where clear direction is necessary. They will be successful entrepreneurs, supervisors, fire chiefs, salespeople, coaches, and athletes. Their determination to get results often makes them come across as aggressive and unfeeling toward others.

When you're trying to influence a driver personality, concentrate your arguments on the results they are trying to get. This person tends to be impatient with details and wants to get to the bottom line as quickly as possible. Instead of building an elaborate case with lots of facts, figures, and specifications, you need to get right to the point. That's what these people are comfortable with, and they're capable of making quick decisions if what you're presenting makes sense to them from a result-oriented point of view.

The fourth type of personality is the *expressive* or *socializer*. This type is both extraverted and people-oriented. Socializers tend to sparkle with energy and personality. They talk rapidly and use emotion and gestures to interact with other people. Socializers are achievement-oriented: they are very interested in themselves and their accomplishments. In order to persuade this personality, concentrate on their achievements and show how they can accomplish even more and gain even greater recognition by following your recommendations.

The most persuasive person is the one who can use all four styles: the one who is flexible in dealing with different personalities. Poor communicators tend to insist upon treating everybody the way they themselves think and act. The excellent communicator takes some time to get a feeling for the other person's responses, motivations, and interests before attempting to persuade or influence. This flexibility is fairly easy to develop if you simply slow down in your communications and watch and listen intently to the other person. Good communicators are good listeners. They develop a sensitivity that enables them to be far more effective in getting cooperation from others.

First impressions are lasting.

The Power of Suggestion

The power of suggestion is another important factor in influencing others. The basic rule is that everything counts. Everything that you do or neglect to do has an impact on whether or not the other person will cooperate with you.

First impressions are lasting. You never get a second chance to make a good first impression. People make judgments about you within the first four seconds of meeting you for the first time. Within thirty seconds, their judgment or opinion of you has been largely set in concrete. In no time at all, they have filed you away into a particular category, and it's very difficult for a person to change his or her mind about you once it's been made up. Once you've come to a conclusion about a person or situation, you naturally tend to look for information that reinforces your conclusion while ignoring information that contradicts it.

For these reasons, it's important to think carefully about the first impressions you make, especially in dress, accessories, posture, grooming, body language, tone of voice, and attitude. Everything counts. If you're going to be making an important presentation or going to an important interview, you'll be more effective if you use mental programming techniques. The most powerful of these is *mental rehearsal*: closing your eyes and visualizing yourself in the situation, seeing yourself as calm, confident, relaxed, and in complete control. Visualize the other person responding to you positively and constructively. Create the exact emotion that would accompany a successful interview or presentation. Get the feeling that goes with a picture of success.

Use mental rehearsal: visualize yourself as calm, confident, and relaxed.

Once you have this mental picture and have emotionalized it, you can relax and drop the entire process into your subconscious mind. From that point onward, your subconscious mind will adjust your behaviors, body language, words, emotions, and actions to make them consistent with the picture that you've programmed into it.

Reciprocity and Obligation

A good deal of research has been done in recent years into the factors that influence people to behave as they do. It's useful to be aware of some of these factors so you can be more effective in guiding other people's behavior on your behalf.

Dr. Robert Cialdini of Arizona State University has identified several influence factors, or what he calls "triggers," that cause people to respond immediately in a favorable way, even when they had no previous interest. These factors are used all the time in sales, marketing, negotiating, and relationships. When you know them, you can both use them on your own behalf and recognize when they're being used on you.

According to Cialdini, the most powerful of all influence factors is *reciprocity* and *obligation*. We're structured psychologically so that whenever anyone does anything for us, we feel obligated to reciprocate. Whenever someone does us a favor, we feel we owe them one in return. Whenever someone makes a concession to us, we feel obligated to make one too. Positive give-and-take in relationships is based on this unspoken but accepted principle.

The Main Influence Factors

- Reciprocity and obligation
- Commitment and consistency
- Social proof
- Liking
- Ethos, pathos, and logos
- Power
- Timing
- Authority
- Scarcity

The most powerful of all influence factors is reciprocity and obligation.

Reciprocity is so powerful that by using it consciously, you can turn a person around 180 degrees, sometimes in seconds.

There are three main forms of reciprocity.

1. *Psychological reciprocity.* For example, if you give a person credit for his or her intelligence, they in turn must give you credit for your intelligence. Always look for ways to trigger this power of psychological reciprocity. Everybody likes a compliment. Sincere compliments often trigger the desire to reciprocate by cooperating with you in helping you to achieve your goals and objectives.

2. *Emotional reciprocity.* If you make another person feel good about himself or herself, that person will feel obligated to make you feel good about yourself. You trigger this factor of emotional reciprocity when you do a favor, when you send a thank-you card or gift, or whenever you do something that is kind or generous for another.

3. *Material reciprocity.* Whenever you do something material or financially for another person, you trigger within them a desire to reciprocate to the same or an even greater extent. If you pay for lunch this week, you trigger the obligation to pay for lunch next week. If you help a person financially, they will feel obligated, consciously and unconsciously, to repay you in some similar fashion. Reciprocity is so powerful that it underlies almost all personal and business relationships. Indeed in the United States, our entire society is based on the law of contract,

which is a formalized method of reciprocity. Successful business-people, salespeople, and politicians continually use reciprocity to trigger the desire to help them.

Commitment and Consistency

The second influence factor that Cialdini identified is *commitment and consistency*. Ralph Waldo Emerson said, "A foolish consistency is the hobgoblin of little minds." In any case, we all try to remain consistent with what we have said or done in the past. We buy the same foods; we go to the same restaurants; we drive the same cars; we follow the same route to work and home; we shop at the same stores; and we make other decisions in the same way.

Whenever you can show a person that what you are asking is consistent with they have done or said in the past, you exert a powerful persuasive influence on that person's behavior. When you're making a sales presentation, for example, if you show the prospect that what you are selling is consistent with what they have said they need or want, it becomes very hard for them to resist your offer.

There is also what I call the *law of incremental commitment*. This says that when you first approach people with a new idea, they have very little commitment to doing it, because they've never done it before. However, people tend to act themselves into commitment. If they take a small action at first, they will tend to take greater actions in the future. You can often influence a person to go along with your suggestion by simply pointing out that what you're asking is quite consistent with what they have already said or done.

You also trigger commitment and consistency when you get a face-to-face meeting with prospective clients. When they have invested time in meeting you, giving you information, and learning about your offerings, they start down the slippery slope of incremental commitment toward becoming full-fledged customers. We act ourselves into commitment little by little; then we strive to remain consistent with what we have done in the recent past.

Social Proof

The third form of persuasion is *social proof.* One of the first things that a person thinks or says when presented with a new idea is, who else has done it? Research shows that we are inordinately influenced to act by learning that someone else similar to ourselves has already done it. We assume that the other person, being as intelligent and discriminating as we are, has carefully evaluated the pros and cons of the offer before making a yes decision.

Liking

Another influence factor is *liking.* Human beings are predominantly emotional. When a person genuinely likes another person, he or she tends to be far more receptive to whatever that person is asking or offering. Emotions distort valuations. When we like the person who's making the offering, we tend to downplay its weaknesses and emphasize its positive factors.

Liking is one of the most powerful of all factors in persuasion. All successful salespeople, negotiators, politicians, and businesspeople tend to be warm, friendly, and genuinely likable. There's probably nothing that will make you more effective in influencing others than to work on your own personality, to build your own self-esteem and self-acceptance, and to convey your inner feelings of self-liking outward toward liking and accepting of other people.

Ethos, Pathos, and Logos

There are three other keys to persuasion, and their names all come from the Greek language: *ethos, pathos,* and *logos.*

Ethos stands for your character, credibility, personality, and your ethics. Whenever you hope to influence anyone else, you first need to establish your credibility: the fact that the other person can trust you and believe in what you are saying. At a public talk, the speaker is introduced with information about their achievements in order to build up their credibility in the minds of the audience. Speakers too often begin by expanding on their credentials and describing their accomplishments to impress the audience and open their minds to listen.

In a professional situation, you must first establish *ethos,* which in this context means your credibility. You can accomplish this by giving some brief background information on yourself or your company. If you wish to sell an idea, for example, you might explain where you acquired the information upon which your conclusions are based. This builds up your credibility and opens up the listener's mind to what you're about to say. The more believable you are, the more likely you are to be persuasive.

The second part of persuasion is *pathos*: connecting with the deep subconscious needs of your listeners. Because people are primarily emotional, you're most likely to persuade them by speaking to their emotional needs.

Think through in advance what needs you can satisfy. It may be the need for prestige, financial gain, security, beauty, health, respect, self-esteem, or personal and professional growth. Good persuaders structure their arguments in such a way that they tap into the key needs of their audience. Addressing the right need triggers a desire in the person to act in the way you are suggesting.

The third part of persuasion is *logos*: logic, or why a person should accept your recommendation. This part of your argument always comes after ethos and pathos, because people use logic, reason, and arguments to confirm decisions they've already made based on their emotions and needs. Successful presenters always remember to keep these three—ethos, pathos, and logos—in their proper order.

The best way to influence others is to put yourself in their position and look at your offering through their eyes. Why would they want to cooperate with you? What are the best arguments that you can marshal to persuade them to accept your recommendation? What do they want or need that you can satisfy? What's in it for them? How will they benefit? People do things for their reasons, not yours.

Power is an important factor in persuading others. Take your time, and get all the information you need before you launch. Be patient; speak to other people. Investigate every source of information that you can find to help your case. The power is always on the side of the person with the best information and the most accurate notes.

Timing

In addition to careful preparation, another important element of persuasion is timing. The Bible says there is a time for every purpose under heaven. There is a too soon and a too late in all of human affairs, and there is a right time and a wrong time to present a case or persuade someone. Picking your time and place can be the most important thing you do in achieving success. When you speak to a person, it's always advisable to ask, "Is this a good time to talk?" If a person is rushed, upset, or distressed, it's much better to delay the conversation and come back at another, more appropriate time. Excellent communicators are sensitive to the psychological and emotional dynamics of a conversation and to whether or not the timing is right for what they're trying to accomplish.

If you're trying to get a person to do something they have never done before, remember that there's tremendous resistance to anything new in the minds of almost everyone. Very few people can accept a new idea or a new way of doing things the first time it's presented; they will respond with resistance, negativity, and just plain no. They're in a comfort zone, and they want to stay there. People will even resist positive and beneficial change rather than move out of their comfort zones.

You can reduce resistance to new ideas by making the other person aware of the problems that exist and showing how adopting your idea can alleviate those problems. Present your idea in the form of a solution with a definite, measurable benefit to the other person. Expect resistance, and be patient. Since some people are motivated by fear, point out the hazards and costs of not accepting your idea. Show how the person can benefit by going ahead and how they will potentially suffer a loss by not doing what you are suggesting. People need time to adjust to new information. It takes about three days for a person to internalize or accept a new idea and begin to see its advantages.

A small pamphlet given to me by a wise man many years ago called "Take Time Out for Mental Digestion" The writer recommended that you present your ideas in a low-key, nonaggressive way. Then knowing that you will get resistance if the idea is new, just leave the idea with the person to think about for two or three days.

Authority

Another influence factor that Cialdini has identified is *authority*. We tend to be strongly influenced by people and publications that we respect as being authorities in their field. For example, the magazine *Consumer Reports* has a powerful authority that determines probably hundreds of millions of dollars' worth of purchases every year. It is seen as an objective magazine giving timely and accurate information on the merits of a great number of products. Many people won't even buy a product before they've read about it in *Consumer Reports*. If, on the other hand, *Consumer Reports* gives a bad rating, that alone can cause that product to go into a tailspin in the market.

In every community, there are business and social leaders who are highly respected by other members of the community. If one of these leaders buys your product or service, that information is often sufficient to cause many others to do the same thing.

Scarcity

The final factor that causes people to act quickly rather than to take their time is *scarcity*. Researchers have found that when something appears to be scarce or hard to get, it becomes far more attractive in the eye of the prospective purchaser. When we were in high school, we didn't even know that we were interested in a particular member of the opposite sex until that person began playing hard to get. Suddenly that person became far more interesting and attractive than before. There's an old saying in selling: "No urgency, no sale." Whenever an item is scarce, it becomes more attractive in the mind and heart of the prospective purchaser.

The takeaway clause is a common technique in selling: The salesperson, confronted with a buyer who cannot make up their mind, suddenly says, "Just a minute. Before we go on, let me check and see if we still have the size and color that you're looking for." The salesperson then goes off to check to make sure that they still have the item in the desired size, color, or shape. Often when the possibility develops that they might not be able to get it at all, an indecisive buyer suddenly decides that they want the item very badly. This technique is commonly used in ladies' boutiques, automobile sales, and even in the purchase of large, expensive homes. Whenever you can suggest that if a person does not act quickly, there may be no chance to get it at all, you can often trigger a decision.

Scarcity implies value. Something that is scarce is considered to be far more desirable, and therefore the decision is far more urgent than if the item is in ample supply and there's no pressure to decide.

A Sample of Cheese

Here's an example that illustrates five of these influence factors in action, all at the same time. You're walking through the supermarket on a Saturday afternoon. Someone stops you and offers you a free sample of cheese. Without thinking, you accept the free sample and eat it. Instantly, the law of reciprocity is triggered: you feel obligated to pay back the person for the free sample by buying a full container of the product, even though a few moments before you were completely uninterested.

Furthermore, eating a little bit of the product triggers the principle of consistency. Now that you have enjoyed a sample, purchasing a full container is consistent with your initial enjoyment. Having taken the first act, you have begun incrementally acting yourself into commitment to a full purchase. If other people around you are also tasting the free samples and buying the full packages, the factor of social proof kicks in: it must be all right for you to do the same.

If the salesperson is pleasant and friendly and thanks you courteously, the influence factor of liking kicks in. You want to buy the item because you feel positive about the salesperson. In addition, if there's information that suggests that this is an exciting new product approved by the store or by *Better Homes and Gardens* or has the Good Housekeeping Seal of Approval, you are influenced by authority.

Virtually all effective advertising and sales appeals use these factors to induce individuals to move from negative or neutral to positive and to acceptance of the product or service.

Action Exercise

Now here's an action exercise for you. What do you need to do to be more effective at persuading others to cooperate with you? Write down a list of the people and situations where it would be helpful to have the cooperation of others. Specify a clear goal for each situation. What do you want to accomplish? What would be the ideal outcome if you were completely successful in getting your way?

Now think through what is in it for the other person. What can you do to establish your credibility and present your idea so that it satisfies their deep subconscious needs? What arguments and logic can you marshal to support your argument? How can you demonstrate that the other person will get the benefit that you're suggesting? Remember, people will only do things for their reasons, not yours.

People will only do things for their reasons, not yours.

You can get almost anything you want if you'll present your ideas and desires in the form of benefits and advantages to the other person. Instead of thinking about what you want, reverse the process: think about what the other person wants and how you can help them get it. You can use these principles with your children, your spouse, your boss, and your customers. You can get more of what you want faster by practicing these persuasion techniques at every opportunity. Try them and see for yourself.

2

Everything Is Negotiable

Your ability to negotiate effectively in your best interests is central to your success. Negotiating and compromising are major parts of the business of living, communicating, and interacting with others. You begin to negotiate in infancy, and you continue to negotiate through to the present moment. It never stops. Life can even be viewed as one extended negotiating session from the cradle to the grave.

Negotiating is just the way in which individuals with differing values and interests find constructive ways to live and work together in harmony. Your ability to negotiate on your own behalf largely determines how well you do in almost every area of your life.

I began studying negotiating many years ago. In the course of my career, I've negotiated many millions of dollars' worth of contracts involving residential, commercial, and industrial real estate. Consequently, the material you're about to learn is based on extensive experience, and it works. If you systematically apply even a small part of what I'm about to spell out, you will greatly improve the quality and quantity of your results.

Negotiating and bargaining have been going on since the beginning of human society. They are how we balance conflicting and competing wants to ensure that each person achieves the best possible outcome for themselves.

Negotiating is rooted in the subjective theory of value, which simply says that *value lies in the eyes of the beholder.* There's no intrinsic value or price on anything—only the price that someone is willing to pay for it. This theory also says that different people place different values on different things at different times and for different reasons. Some will value money more than goods and services, while others will value the goods and services more than the money. These subjective valuations create the desire to exchange goods, services, and money in the first place. As they say, it is differences of opinion that make a horse race.

Value lies in the eyes of the beholder.

No Price Is Fixed

This brings us to the first basic principle of successful negotiating: everything is negotiable. There are very few fixed prices or terms on anything that you want to purchase—even if they're written down in the boldest, blackest letters.

The average person who goes to purchase any item naturally tends to believe that if a price is written down, it must be fixed in some way. However, all prices are subjective. They are the best-guess estimate of what the market will bear at a particular time. In many cases, the written prices are not even meant to be taken seriously; they're simply put there as the starting point for bargaining.

Negotiating to get the best price or the best deal is part of the game of life. As long as you look upon it as a game, you can avoid getting tense or nervous in a negotiating situation. Simply smile to yourself, get in there, and play the game.

The key to negotiating and getting better prices and terms is *simply to ask.* You can ask politely, you can ask innocently, you can ask curiously, but be sure to ask. Ask why the price is so high. Ask for better terms. Ask for more for the same price, ask for a better deal or a lower price. Because all prices are arbitrarily set by someone in the back room or head office, all prices are subject to negotiation in some way and on some basis.

Develop the attitude that all prices are negotiable, and continually look for opportunities to improve each deal in your favor. One of the fastest ways to achieve financial success is to pay less for the things that you buy and get more for the things that you sell. A good bargainer or negotiator can earn as much net income in five years as a poor negotiator might earn in twenty years of equally hard work.

The primary reason people are not better negotiators is the fear of rejection.

The primary reason people are not better negotiators is the fear of rejection. We're conditioned from childhood to be sensitive to the acceptance and approval of other people. If we feel that asking for a better price may cause the other person to become upset or express disapproval of us, we often accept the written price passively and end up by paying far more than we need to.

Don't Let Rejection Hold You Back

The key to overcoming the fear of rejection is to confront it by practicing over and over. Develop the habit of looking upon every interchange as a negotiation, and just practice. Here's an example of what I mean. A few years ago in February, I went into the most expensive menswear store in the city, and I was looking at a beautiful cashmere coat. I tried it on, and it fit perfectly. The price tag on the coat said $500, but it had been reduced to $350, probably because the winter was half over. I decided to see if I could get an even better deal on this lovely coat. When the clerk came over, I told him that I liked the coat. He told me that it was the last one in stock. I told him that I would like to buy it, but that $350 was too much.

He told me that there was nothing he could do about it, because the price was fixed as written on the price tag.

I realized that he had no authority to reduce the price, so I made him an offer. I said, "I'll give you $200 cash for the coat today, but I must have a decision by 2:00 p.m. this afternoon." He again replied that there was no way they could sell the coat for a penny less than $350.

I then told him, "Why don't you go and talk to your manager?" He was at lunch at the time. "I'll give you my telephone number. If you decide to accept the $200, please contact me within the next two hours at this number."

I went back to my apartment and waited. Ninety minutes later, the telephone rang, and the clerk, sounding quite surprised, told me that the coat was mine for $200.

When I went over to pick it up, he was still somewhat surprised: in all the time that he'd been working at the store, he had never seen it vary from their posted prices. In fact, he said no one had ever offered a price lower than the ones on the tags. He shook my hand and congratulated me on having gotten a terrific deal.

The point I'm making is that often the clerk you're speaking to is not aware that the prices are negotiable. Often you'll have to go over his or her head to the manager to arrange a better deal. Don't be afraid to do so. If you make a lower offer or ask for a lower price, the worst thing that can happen is that the manager will say no. In most cases, he or she will counteroffer. As a last resort, do what I did: give a fixed offer along with your telephone number and a deadline for acceptance. It's amazing how flexible a company can be when they have the choice of making a small profit or none at all.

Hallmarks of a Successful Negotiator

Here are the hallmarks of a successful negotiator: This is a person who continually looks for creative ways to move the price terms or situation in his or her favor. Successful negotiators view negotiation as a lifelong process, an ongoing, never-ending part of interacting and exchanging with other people. They see negotiations going on everywhere, from the time they get up in the morning and negotiate with the family for the bathroom or the kitchen to negotiating all day long while working with other people. Successful negotiators see bargaining, trading, and compromising contained in all human interaction and exchange. Successful negotiators are open-minded, adaptive, and creative. They are willing to consider all types of options and possibilities in approaching a negotiating situation.

Successful negotiators regard negotiation as a lifelong process.

Successful negotiators avoid taking fixed positions or digging in their heels with nonnegotiable demands. Successful negotiators are fluid and flexible. They are quick to identify mutual goals and look for areas of compromise early on to get the negotiations off to a smooth start. They are cooperative rather than competitive. The most successful negotiators continually seek for collaborative solutions to problems, looking for ways to come to agreements that are beneficial to both parties. They look continually for newer, easier, innovative, and unusual ways to help both parties get what they want. Finally, successful negotiators are honest, direct, and nonmanipulative. They emphasize the value of the relationship and the importance of good relations between the two parties both during and after the negotiations.

This brings us to Gerard Nierenberg's definition of the purpose of negotiating: to reach an agreement such that all parties have their needs satisfied to the degree to which they are internally motivated to fulfill their commitments and enter into subsequent negotiations and transactions with the same party.

That is a real mouthful, so let's break it down into its important parts. First, the purpose of negotiating is to reach an agreement such that all parties have their needs satisfied. This means that no one goes away from the negotiation feeling that he or she has suffered or been taken advantage of in any way. The agreement meets all of the critical needs of both parties.

Second, the purpose of negotiating is to reach an agreement such that all parties are internally motivated to fulfill their commitments. That is, both parties are strongly committed to carrying through with what they've agreed to do. If the negotiation has ended with acceptable solutions to the needs of both parties, they will be eager to fulfill their commitments in order to benefit from the fruits of the negotiation.

Finally, the purpose of negotiation is to reach an agreement such that both parties will enter into subsequent negotiations and transactions with the same party in the future. If you've negotiated successfully, you will have laid the groundwork for future successful negotiations, which may go on for many years. In fact, the most successful businesspeople and negotiators in America have built their careers and fortunes on a network of business relationships where negotiations have taken place over and over again throughout their careers.

A good negotiator thinks of the third and the fourth negotiation with the other party while he or she is involved in the first. This attitude creates a desire within both parties to enter into agreements that both can happily and comfortably live with for the long term.

Six Styles of Agreement

The six basic styles of agreement are described by many authorities on negotiating but are perhaps best explained in Stephen Covey's book *Seven Habits of Highly Effective People*. Be aware of these various styles of negotiating so you can select the style that's most appropriate to your long-term goals.

The first is called *win-lose negotiating*. This is very common. It's the type of negotiating in which you get what you want while the

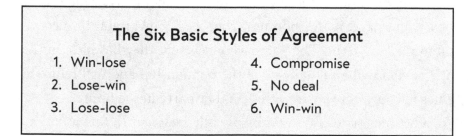

The Six Basic Styles of Agreement

1. Win-lose   4. Compromise
2. Lose-win   5. No deal
3. Lose-lose   6. Win-win

other person does not. You are satisfied, if not oversatisfied, with the result, but the other party is not satisfied at all. As you can see, this violates the purpose of negotiating described above. If the second party leaves a negotiation dissatisfied, they will have no desire to enter into subsequent negotiations with you because they will feel that they have lost. In a win-lose negotiation, the advantage is usually only temporary. Avoid entering into this type of arrangement even when you have the power to do so.

The second type of negotiation is *lose-win*. This is when the other party gets what they want, but *you* fail to get what you want, so you leave the negotiation dissatisfied. Many people allow themselves to be railroaded into lose-win negotiations for fear of confrontation or offending the other party.

Psychologically manipulative people make a habit of putting others into lose-win situations, knowing that most people prefer to be accommodating rather than competitive or confrontative. Do not allow anyone in your personal or business life to put you into a lose-win situation. When this happens, a dynamic is created that makes it very likely that it will happen again.

A lose-win situation is often accompanied by intimidation, ultimatums, and threats to do or not do something to or for you. Such a situation can arise if one person values the relationship more than the other and the other takes advantage of this difference.

Both win-lose and lose-win forms of reaching agreement may benefit one party in the short term, but they're invariably unsuccessful in the long term. The party who feels that they have lost in the negotiation will eventually leave the relationship and will refuse to enter into any agreement with the other party in the future.

The third style of negotiating is called *lose-lose*. In this situation, neither party gets what they want. Often people get into what is called *positional bargaining*, where they dig in on their positions and invest their egos in being right and winning. When this happens, the two parties would rather not come to an agreement at all rather than come to one where the other party might benefit. When egos get in the way, the two parties will often argue, disagree, and finally settle on a solution that pleases neither of them. Most lose-lose agreements are accompanied by high levels of emotional involvement by both parties. When you see yourself getting into a lose-lose negotiation, it's time to stand back and get your ego out of the way.

The fourth style of negotiating is *compromise*. In a compromise, some wants of each party are fulfilled, but some are left unfulfilled. Both parties are partially satisfied and partially dissatisfied. We often enter into compromise agreements to avoid conflict or reach some conclusion so that we can get on with something else. Compromises may or may not be satisfactory, but they tend to leave certain unresolved issues, which may come up later, causing further conflict and further negotiation.

The fifth style of negotiating is simply called *no deal*. The two parties to the negotiation agree to disagree. They can't reach a happy meeting ground where both are satisfied and have their essential needs met, so they agree not to enter into an agreement at all. This is not particularly productive, but it does have the advantage of avoiding a negative situation that would make it difficult or impossible for the two parties to enter into further negotiations at another time. The no deal outcome occurs most commonly when you're shopping around for an item, hiring someone, applying for a job, or merely rejecting an offer to buy or sell something.

The sixth style is called *win-win* negotiating. This is a mature, rational process whereby two parties collaborate and cooperate to find a solution—often a third alternative to the positions of either—that satisfies the needs of both.

Here are some typical examples of these methods of negotiating. Take a couple who are negotiating on where to go for their summer vacation. He wants to go to the mountains, and she wants to go to the seashore. He doesn't particularly like the beach, and she doesn't particularly like the mountains. In a win-lose negotiation (from the husband's point of view), he would insist, and they would end up going to the mountains. He would be happy, and she would be dissatisfied. In a lose-win negotiation (again from the husband's point of view), to keep the peace, they go to the seashore. She has her needs met, but he is left dissatisfied. In a lose-lose negotiation, they would go to neither the seashore nor the mountains but would instead visit their in-laws. Neither party would be satisfied: both would lose with no advantage for either.

In a compromise negotiation, the couple would go to the seashore for half of their vacation and to the mountains for the other half. Each party would get something but would be dissatisfied for half the time. This is the weakness in compromises: satisfaction is never fully guaranteed to either party. If they decide to do a no-deal negotiation, they could agree to disagree. They could decide not to go on vacation at all that year, or she could go to the seashore and he could go to the mountains on separate vacations. Each would be partly satisfied, but no happy solution would have been found.

In a win-win negotiation, the couple would seek out a third alternative that would satisfy the needs of both. They might, for example, decide to visit Vancouver, British Columbia, where the mountains meet the sea. Downtown Vancouver is only twenty minutes from the mountains and fifteen minutes from the beach. She could go to the beach all day while he went to the mountains, and they could get together each evening. Both would have their major needs satisfied, and they would still be taking their summer vacation together and enjoying each other's company.

In my experience, a third alternative is almost always available to two parties who feel that they have reached an impasse. If you look long enough and hard enough in the right spirit, you can usually find a way to reach a win-win agreement of some kind.

This is the key: *your attitude must be win-win or no deal.* You must be committed to finding a solution that satisfies the basic needs of both parties, or you must agree to disagree. In any case, you will not accept a win-lose, lose-win, lose-lose, or compromise solution. It will be win-win or no deal. When you start from that point of view, you'll be amazed at how much more readily you will move toward win-win solutions.

The material I'm presenting in this book, by the way, is based on the win-win model. All of the strategies, tactics, and techniques that you will learn here will be geared toward moving toward genuine win-win solutions.

Critical Elements

Here are some of the critical elements in successful win-win negotiating.

The first is *power.* No one will seriously negotiate with you unless they feel you have the power to help them get something they want or the power to hurt them in some way. Power is a critical factor in all interactions and negotiations between two people who want something from each other.

Whether or not you genuinely have power, it's important to create the perception of having it. One way is by appearing to be indifferent to whether or not the negotiation works out. A person who appears uninterested or indifferent in a negotiation always has a psychological edge over one for whom the outcome is ostensibly more important.

You can also convey the perception of power by real or implied scarcity. For example, if you're selling something, you can say or imply that you have only one or a few left and that they'll soon all be sold, no matter what the other party agrees to at this time. You can control a scarce and desired product, service, or item, which gives you an element of power.

You can create the perception of power by conveying authority: you dress, carry yourself, and have a title that seems to give you enormous authority. This perception can be very persuasive.

You can also create the perception of power through courage. When you seem to be willing to take a risk or go out on a limb, it creates a perception which often causes the other party to deal with you more seriously.

Elements of Power Negotiating

Six major forms of power are used in negotiating. It's important to be aware of them so that you can use them when appropriate and avoid being the victim of them if they're used on you.

The first power is the power of *commitment*. A person who is most committed and determined to working out a deal has a power that the person who is wishy-washy or unsure lacks. One who is committed and determined to make a sale is a far more formidable opponent in a negotiation than a person who has not thought about it or who is hesitant.

The second power is *expertise*. A person with superior knowledge and recognized expertise in the field—such as a medical or legal

---

Six Elements of Power Negotiating

- Commitment
- Expertise
- Knowledge of the other's needs
- Identification or empathy
- Reward or punishment
- Investment

---

specialist, an engineer, or architect—has a tremendous amount of power in a negotiation. What he or she says carries a lot more weight than the position of someone who lacks expertise. Even quoting a recognized expert or carrying some written statement or proof by such an expert can give you power in a negotiating situation.

The third type of power is *knowledge of the needs of the other.* The person who knows what the other person wants and needs better has a special form of power in a negotiation.

The fourth is the power of *identification* or *empathy* with the other party. Your ability to form a warm relationship based on trust, empathy, and understanding gives you a tremendous edge in a negotiation. A person who really likes you is much more amenable to working out a solution that is agreeable to both of you.

The fifth form of power is the power of *reward* or *punishment*: having the ability to do or not do something for the other person. A boss, for example, has the power to raise the wages of, promote, demote, or fire a subordinate. When you negotiate with a person who can either reward or punish you, it's important to develop viable options and alternatives so that you have something to fall back on. Otherwise, you're at the mercy of the person with this power.

The sixth and final form of power is the power of *investment.* The more time and money that either party has invested in the negotiation, the more likely it is that the parties will be willing to compromise to achieve an agreement. When a negotiation begins, neither party has a lot at stake. However, the more time, the more money, and the more energy invested in going back and forth, the more each of the parties will have at stake.

The Power of Desire

This brings us to another key element in negotiating: *desire*. Desire is a critical determinant of what happens in a negotiation. How badly do you want the outcome? How badly does the other party want it? The person who gets the most emotionally involved in a negotiation is the one who has the least power in that negotiation.

Chinese jade merchants are famous for their technique of showing only one piece of jewelry at a time. They can always tell when they've shown a piece that the prospective customer finds particularly attractive: the customer's eyes light up. No matter how blank the face of the prospective customer, the merchants are trained to watch for the dilation of the pupils. They're then prepared to negotiate only for the sale of that particular piece. When you intensely desire to purchase something, you often give it away in your face, your body, your tone of voice, or your behavior. It's therefore important to practice detachment, especially with an emotional purchase, such as a house or a car.

This brings us to what I call the *walkaway method of negotiation*. This is a very useful technique, based on my discovery while living in Mexico and bargaining in the marketplace: you never know the lowest price until you turn to walk away. I can remember negotiating for a piece of gold jewelry in Puerto Vallarta, Mexico. I didn't get the merchant down low enough, so I used the walkaway technique: I walked out of the store and kept walking. I really wanted the jewelry, but I realized that if I hesitated or turned around, I would lose. As I got a full block away, the merchant, who had been watching me, his eyes boring into my back, finally broke and came running after to sell me the jewelry at the last price I had offered.

There are many ways to use the walkaway technique. The critical part is your mental attitude: if you're going to get the best deal, you must be prepared to walk away. You must be prepared to give up your investment in time, emotion, energy, even money, and walk out of the negotiation if that's what it takes. You must be prepared to go through with your threat to leave and never come back. You can only use this method when you have excellent information about the cost structure and competitive pricing of what you're trying to buy. But being prepared to walk away gives you tremendous bargaining strength for any item, large or small, for which there are many suppliers and therefore a very competitive market. Try it yourself and see.

Time and Options

Another important element in negotiating is *time*. There's a big difference between a negotiation conducted within tight time constraints and one that is conducted with all the time in the world. There's an old saying: no urgency, no sale. Imply that you have all the time in the world and you're in no rush to make any decision. The more time you appear to have, the more advantage you have in negotiating price and terms. It's also to your advantage to set a deadline for a decision whenever possible. Often, if you give people a very short period of time to make up their minds one way or the other, they will move to a decision quickly rather than drawing it out. Conversely, you should avoid being rushed in any way. It's hard to make a decision or negotiate the best agreement when you're under time constraints.

The most important element in negotiating is the number of options that you have to the subject of the negotiation: the more you have, the better off you are. Your strength lies in developing as many alternatives as possible before going into the negotiation. If you have no choice but to settle for one item, you have no freedom at all. In fact, a rule for happiness in life is that you are free in direct proportion to the number of options that you have developed.

A good way to develop options is to sit down with a pad of paper and use the twenty-idea method. At the top of the page, write the question: "What alternatives do I have if this negotiation fails completely?" Then force yourself to write ten to twenty answers to that question.

Knowing that you have lots of alternatives will give you a tremendous psychological edge in a negotiation. Make clear goals for each negotiating situation: you must know what you want, and you must know what you are prepared to give to get it. Clarity is essential. Clearly think through the alternatives in advance, and think on paper. Define your ideal outcome: write out a description of exactly what you would like to happen if the negotiation succeeds completely as you would like it. Discuss this ideal outcome with others to get their input and feedback. The person who is perfectly clear about what he or she wants has a powerful advantage over the one who is vague or unsure.

In clarifying what you want, it's advisable to develop three numbers, especially if you're buying or selling something: (1) the highest and the best that you think you can get; (2) what you would settle for, a medium or middle-range figure; (3) the lowest amount that you would accept, the worst possible outcome; you would hate to have to accept this amount, but if necessary, you would go along with it.

These numbers represent your *opening position*, your *fallback position*, and your *final fallback position* respectively. The more time you've spent in thinking through these figures, the more effective you will be. You'll always know where you are. You can open with a number that is slightly higher than your ideal, and you know that you will never accept less than your final fallback position, so you can negotiate confidently within that range.

Preparation is the key to successful negotiating. Perhaps 80 percent of the success of a negotiation is determined by the quality and quantity of the preparation you do beforehand. You need to prepare several items before you begin to negotiate, especially when it's expensive or important:

1. The subject matter: exactly what is to be discussed. What is the subject of the negotiation? Many people go into negotiations without knowing the reason for it in the first place.

2. Objectives. What are your objectives in the negotiation? What are the other party's objectives? Sometimes, calling them to ask what they expect to get will give you a tremendous amount of information. Calling other people who are aware of the situation can also give you valuable insights. What are the issues to be discussed? Where do you differ from the other party in your wants and needs? Where are the potential areas of conflict and debate?

3. Positions. What are the starting positions of each party? What are you and the other party likely to lead off with as initial demands?

Negotiating Positions

Positions are usually the starting point in a negotiating situation. Positions are made up of your essentials, your limits, your maximums, and your minimums. What must you get from this negotiation? What does the other party want? In which areas are you inflexible, and in which areas are you willing to concede? Where can you make concessions without damaging what you feel you must get from this negotiation? Take a piece of paper and draw a line down the center. In the left-hand column, write all of your musts, the things you must achieve with this negotiation. In the right-hand column, make a list of all of your wants or things that would be nice to accomplish. Keep the two lists clear in your mind when you're negotiating.

And finally with regard to positioning, what tie-in concessions can you require to achieve agreement or get concessions from the other party? If you're willing to give up on some things, what can you ask for in return? Can you ask for a better price, better terms, better delivery? Can you ask for certain things to be added or deleted from the final package?

A valuable exercise in preparing for negotiations is what lawyers do in preparing a case before they go to court: arguing the case from the other person's viewpoint. They put themselves in the position of the other lawyer and prepare the other lawyer's case from beginning to end. Only then do they go to work to prepare their own case, having carefully thought out everything that might possibly happen in the courtroom.

If you practice empathy, you can begin to see the negotiation through the eyes of the other person. You can make a list of all the things that you think they want or need to achieve in this negotiation. That can be your starting point for preparing what you will concede and what you will ask.

Perhaps the most important part of this entire discussion on preparation is having the discipline to sit down with a pad and paper and clearly think through what you are trying to accomplish before you begin. Many misunderstandings arise in negotiating, and errant assumptions lie at the root of most mistakes. A major reason for misunderstanding is false or incorrect assumptions held by both parties through a lack of clarity.

It's a useful exercise to think through both your known and your hidden assumptions. One assumption, for example, that we tend to have when entering into a negotiation is that the other party wants to reach an agreement. Often this assumption is false. Sometimes we assume that the other party has either more or less information than we provide. False assumptions can damage both negotiations and relationships. Ask yourself, what if my assumptions were not true? Examine your most cherished or important assumptions. What if they weren't true at all? What if the product or service is not as good as it seemed to be? What if the price is not as reasonable as it appears? What if the other person is not negotiating in good faith? Be willing to be brutally frank in challenging your pet assumptions. This is the mark of the skilled thinker and the excellent negotiator.

False assumptions can damage both negotiations and relationships.

Once you've identified your assumptions, how can you test them? How can you gather information to ensure that your assumptions are based on fact rather than fantasy?

Sometimes a little effort in testing assumptions can be extremely valuable in bringing a negotiation to a successful conclusion that is in your favor. What are the assumptions of the other person? On what basis are they negotiating? Do they have assumptions that may or may not be correct? How could you find out what their assumptions are? How can you clarify each other's assumptions?

This is an excellent question. If you're working toward a cooperative, win-win negotiating solution, then it's natural to sit down in advance and clarify each other's assumptions so that you're both negotiating from the same basis. The best way to do this is to use the fact-finding approach: sit down and ask questions. Gather data objectively as though you were doing an interview for a newspaper.

Make out a list of your questions. Ask them, and share your answers, as well as your assumptions, with the other party. When they tell you what they are thinking or feeling, feed it back in your own words; paraphrase until the other person agrees that you do understand where they are coming from.

A good question to ask at the beginning is, why do you feel we are here, and what would you ideally like to accomplish in this meeting? If you begin with this question, you can often clarify each other's assumptions and negotiate from a better foundation.

Suggestive Elements

There are also several suggestive elements in negotiating that you should bear in mind, especially in a tricky or difficult negotiation.

As we've already seen, the power of suggestion is inordinately strong in shaping the way people think, feel, and react. Some psychologists have estimated that as much as 95 percent of our thoughts and feelings at any given time are determined by our external environment and what is going on around us—especially in the external human environment.

A key suggestive element in a negotiation is location: where it takes place. It's always preferable to have the negotiation in your office or at your home. You have a psychological advantage when a person comes onto your turf, because you are familiar and comfortable with the terrain. If someone invites you to negotiate on their premises and you can't counter by having them come to yours, you can suggest a neutral space, such as a restaurant or a hotel. Almost all major negotiations are conducted in a place that is satisfactory to both parties.

A second suggestive element is the personality of the negotiator. A warm, friendly, and supportive individual has a much more positive effect on the other party than a negative, cold, or distant person. The more empathetic and sensitive you are, the easier it is for the other person to negotiate with you and concede on minor and even major points.

A third suggestive element is the positioning of the various parties. The traditional group negotiating setup, where the parties sit on opposite sides of the table, often makes reaching an agreement very difficult. During the Paris Peace Talks between the United States and North Vietnam in the 1970s, months of negotiating went on over the size and shape of the tables at which the negotiators would sit. The North Vietnamese were very aware of the importance of positioning around the table in making symbolic statements about the relative power and authority of each party.

The best positioning for a negotiation is at a round table, with both parties sitting side by side. Whenever possible, try to avoid sitting face-to-face or opposite the other party. If several people are involved, a good way to break down the psychological barriers is to alternate the members of each team around the table so that they're spread throughout the room. At the very least, always seek to sit next to your major negotiating opponent. This implies cooperation and conciliation rather than competition and an adversarial relationship.

The fourth key suggestive element in negotiating is timing. A relaxed negotiation with apparently all the time in the world is far different from a negotiation that's rushed, with one party or the other having to be somewhere else in a short time. Never allow yourself to be rushed. If there's not enough time to conclude the negotiation satisfactorily, be willing to delay its completion to another day, when there's more time. It's common for manipulative negotiators to use time urgency as a weapon in their favor.

A fifth key suggestive element of negotiating is comfort. The comfort of the chairs, the level of fatigue, the amount of hunger, thirst, or jet lag that one party or the other is suffering are key elements in a negotiation. A negotiation is always helped when one party is solicitous of the physical needs of the other.

The sixth suggestive element is attitude. A negotiator with a positive, cheerful, and optimistic attitude is much more inviting to reach agreement with than one who is negative or abrasive. One of the most important parts of a positive attitude is the willingness to be calm and patient throughout the negotiations. In my experience, the best negotiators tend to be very low-key, patient, and even gentle men and women. This attitude goes a long way toward relaxing the other party and making them amenable to their suggestions.

One final point on the suggestive influences of negotiating: all negotiations proceed better after or during a meal. When people are hungry, they naturally tend to be irritable and uncooperative, but when they have eaten, they experience a well-being that bodes well for successful negotiating.

Negotiating Complex Agreements

For negotiating a complex agreement, start off by getting an agreement on as many small items as possible before settling down to hammer out the more difficult issues. I've personally negotiated several multimillion dollar real estate contracts. Whenever I've sat down with the negotiators from the other side to go through a fifty- or sixty-page contract, my method has always been to go through it clause by clause, discussing and getting agreement on each area where we have no difficulties. Whenever we come to a clause or to a sticking point where there is a difference of opinion and a need to negotiate some satisfactory compromise, I say, "Let's come back to that later." This method—agreeing on everything about which you can possibly agree before negotiating areas of differences—is always the most effective. The more small agreements that you can reach at the beginning of a negotiation, the more likely you are to reach agreement on the larger issues later.

On every issue where money or concessions are involved, you should agree slowly and reluctantly, but with reasonableness and fairness. I always lace the negotiation with concessions that I describe as fair to everyone involved. The more you can set a tone of fairness throughout the negotiation, the less likely the other party is to be unreasonable about the main issues.

A Harvard study concluded that the most satisfactory way to negotiate opposing points of view was tit for tat: for every concession, the other party should expect an equal and opposite concession. Whenever you make a concession in any area, you should, as a matter of principle, request an equal concession in some other area. If you don't, the other party will place too little value on what you're giving up.

Another technique you can use is called *persuasion by social proof.* This simply means that people are swayed in their opinions by learning of other people like themselves who have entered into the same agreement that you are suggesting now. Whenever you use facts, numbers, names, and statistics from reputable sources to show that others are making similar agreements, you are using persuasion by social proof. This is a very powerful technique, because you are demonstrating the reasonableness and fairness of your position. Again, this is a matter of careful advance preparation so that you have the proof at your fingertips at the critical moment.

Remember, though, that assertions are not proof. What you say is not usually accepted as proof in a negotiation. You must have validation in the form of printed material, testimonial letters, names, or lists of others that can be used as proof or referrals in order to sway the negotiation in your favor.

Bamboozled by a Secretary

Let me give you an example. Many years ago, we hired a secretary at $800 per month. She was young and needed the work, and she had just left a job paying slightly less. We had just opened an office, and we needed someone to take care of the telephones, typing, bank deposits, and other miscellaneous details. The young woman we hired was twenty-two years old. She did an excellent job and whipped our little operation into shape within a couple of months. At that point, as an expression of appreciation, I called her in and gave her an increase from $800 to $1,000 per month, for which she was duly grateful.

Not long after that, we bought a Macintosh computer. She immediately taught herself how to use it and began doing all of our workbooks and correspondence on it. As our accounting became more complex, she taught herself how to do basic accounting, bookkeeping, and monthly financial statements, and she took over that part of the business also.

After she'd been with me for about six months, she asked if she could speak to me about her salary. I knew that she was going to ask for an increase. I was feeling very big-hearted because of the fine job she was doing, I decided that I would give her an increase of 15 percent, or an extra $150 per month, bringing her salary to $1,150 or an increase of approximately 45 percent in the six months since she had begun. I thought that she would be quite happy with this amount.

The secretary came in, closed the door, sat down, and told me that she felt that she deserved an increase. I responded by telling her that I agreed and I was going to give her an extra $150 per month. She replied by saying that she appreciated the thought, but that she had been doing her homework in the marketplace. She had spoken to three personnel agencies and had checked among her friends to find out what a person performing her functions would be paid in another company. She concluded that her job was worth between $1,500 and $1,600 per month based on the work that she was doing.

I couldn't believe it. She was sitting there asking for an increase of more than 50 percent after only six months on the job. As I sat there looking at her and she sat there looking at me, I suddenly realized two things: First, she was definitely worth the extra money, and it would probably cost me $1,500 to replace her, plus the inconvenience involved if she decided to walk away.

The second thing I realized was that I had just been royally outnegotiated by a twenty-two-year-old woman. I had negotiated millions of dollars' worth of contracts with some of the most sophisticated businesspeople in America, and I had just been bamboozled out of a 50 percent increase by this secretary because she had followed proper negotiating procedure: she'd gone out into the marketplace and done her homework. She had prepared carefully and planned the timing so that I would be in the office for several hours, not rushed, and willing and able to sit and talk with her. She'd prepared the environment: she had someone else taking care of the telephones and closed the door behind her. She didn't tell me that she wanted a 50 percent increase because she needed the money. She told me that she wanted a 50 percent increase because on the basis of market statistics (which I hadn't checked and therefore couldn't confirm or deny), she was entitled to the extra money.

As it happened, I gave her the increase she asked for. Only afterwards did I realize how cleverly she had conducted the negotiation.

The reason I tell this story is that one of the fastest ways to move up the financial ladder in your career is to get an increase and be paid substantially more than you're earning today by becoming a good negotiator.

This secretary did all the right things. She made herself more valuable in the areas that were critical for the ongoing survival of our business. She accepted additional responsibility. She took computer courses in the evenings and on the weekends so that she could operate our Macintosh. She got her own instruction at night school on bookkeeping and accounting. She saw the opportunity to make herself virtually indispensable to our company, and she acted on the opportunity. When she was ready to ask for an increase, there was only one thing that we could do, and that was to give it to her. She was worth every penny.

Negotiating Tactics for Purchases

There are several negotiating tactics that you can use if you're attempting to purchase something for the lowest possible price. Make a habit of using these tactics even if the price is apparently reasonable. You'll be amazed at how much you can save on your day-to-day and month-to-month purchases using these simple methods.

The first is called the *flinch*. When a price is mentioned, flinch as though you have just suffered a physical shock and let your face express your amazement at the price. The very act of being surprised and shocked that the price is that high will often cause the seller to drop the price in an instant. When I traveled throughout the world, I found that the first flinch often drops the price by as much as 50 percent. You can use this flinch tactic when buying any expensive item, especially cars, appliances, stereo equipment, and definitely real estate—or any purchase where the price has been set arbitrarily. Remember, people almost always ask for more than they really expect to get.

The second tactic is simply to question. After you've flinched and the prices come down, you ask, "Can't you do better than that?" Sometimes when you're in a store, the clerk will shrug and say, "That's the price, and I can't do anything about it. I don't set the prices." In a case like this, always ask, "Is this item ever on sale?" If the clerk tells you that the item is occasionally on sale, ask how much it sells for when it's reduced. When you get that price, use the walkaway close by offering that price today only, and ask him or her to take it to the manager. Sometimes the manager will say no, in which case you simply leave your name, phone number, and tell them that you'll wait for twenty-four hours before you purchase it somewhere else. You'll be surprised at how often the phone will ring and the price will come down.

A third tactic in buying is simply to tell the person that no matter what the price is, you can get it cheaper somewhere else. The salesperson will be surprised and hurt to hear you say this, but if they think you can get it cheaper somewhere else, they will often be amenable to dropping the price for you today.

Another question you can use after you've been negotiating and you don't seem to be able to get the price down any lower is to ask, "What's the very best you can do if I make a decision today?" Whatever the person says in response, you haven't committed to buying it, and whatever the answer is, "Ask, is that the very best you can do? Can't you do better than that?" Don't be afraid to ask for a lower price. No one is going to sell you anything except at a profit, so the lower the price you can get, the better off you'll be without hurting anyone else.

Another price negotiating tactic is simply to make a lowball offer. Many real estate speculators will make offers on homes for sale at 50 and 60 percent of the asking price. They play the law of averages. They may make a hundred offers, 99 percent of which are thrown back at them, but the hundredth offer is accepted for a variety of reasons: the sellers may be desperate for cash; they may be going through a divorce; they may be moving overseas. In any event, they will sometimes accept the first lowball offer that comes along.

The sixth negotiating tactic is the *nibble* or *add-on*. Just after you've purchased a suit, but before you've taken out your credit card to pay for it, you ask the salesperson to throw in a shirt or a silk tie. After you've made an offer on the house, you ask the seller to throw in all the lawn mowing equipment, the garden furniture, drapes, and a few other things. This tactic is a way to be sure that you get everything that you have coming from every purchase. One of the most common add-ons is, when you buy something large, to ask them to include the cost of the shipping, freight, or delivery in the price. If they refuse, pick up your credit card and say, "Never mind. I'll get it somewhere else," and head for the door. It's doubtful that they'll let you get to the parking lot for the cost of a little freight.

The seventh negotiating tactic that you can use is what is called *an agent without authority.* This means that you can *take* concessions, but you have no authority to *make* concessions. You say that you have to discuss it with your boss, your board of directors, or your spouse, or you have to run it past your accountant or your lawyer. You can negotiate from a position of strength as an agent without authority, because all the other person can do is make concessions, while all that you can do is to accept them.

Be alert to having any of these techniques used against you. If a person says they cannot make a decision without reference to someone else, refuse to continue negotiations until that person is available. Often you'll find that this is merely a negotiating tactic and that this person can make any decision that he or she wants.

Finally, remember that no negotiation is ever final. You are always entitled to change your mind or to rethink a negotiation. If you feel in retrospect that you've entered into a bad deal, don't be shy about going back to the original party and reopening the negotiations. Be willing to say, "I made a mistake" or "I changed my mind." If upon reflection you feel uncomfortable or uneasy about the deal, pick up the telephone, call the person, and simply say, "I'm not happy with this agreement that we entered into. I would like to discuss it with you again and change some of the terms that we negotiated."

Even if you have a signed contract, don't be shy about going back and asking for a change in the terms and conditions. All that the other person can say is no. If you can suggest concessions that you'll make in exchange for the ones that you're requesting, most serious businesspeople will be open to renegotiating an agreement to ensure that both parties are satisfied.

If you want anyone to do something for you, put yourself in their position first and ask how you can do something for them. Remember, the purpose of negotiation is to come to an agreement in such a way that both parties are committed to fulfilling their parts of the agreement and are willing and eager to enter into subsequent negotiations with the same party. If anything happens to threaten or interfere with this purpose, feel free to reopen the negotiation and ask for changes in the terms and conditions.

Four Essentials of Negotiation

You can become an excellent negotiator if you remember the four essentials of negotiating:

1. Get the facts. Prepare in advance. Do your homework beforehand.
2. Ask for what you want. Be clear about your objectives, and be sure to ask clearly and ask persistently for exactly what you want.
3. Seek win-win solutions at all times. Think about negotiating with this person again and again over the years. Make sure that both of you are fully satisfied with the result, even after having slept on it over twenty-four hours.
4. Take every opportunity possible to practice. When your children ask you for something, practice negotiating concessions from them in return. When your spouse asks you to do something, practice negotiating something in return.

Four Essentials of Negotiating

· Prepare in advance.

· Ask for what you want.

· Seek for win-win solutions.

· Take every opportunity to practice.

When your boss, your customers, your suppliers, or your salespeople ask you for something or try to sell you something, make a habit of always negotiating to get a better deal. Always look for a way to reorganize the terms and conditions so as to improve your results. If you persist, prepare, and practice, you will become an excellent negotiator, and you'll be able to negotiate your way to maximum performance and achievement.

An Exercise

Here's an exercise for you: make a list of those areas in your life where you feel that the deal you have gotten or are getting is not satisfactory.

Pick the area or areas where your dissatisfaction is causing you to feel negative or unhappy. Then sit down and, using what you have learned from this chapter, work out a plan to renegotiate the situation in such a way that it satisfies your essential needs. Be sure to structure it so that it is win-win for all parties concerned.

From this point on, whenever you feel that you are not getting a fair deal, resolve to go back in and renegotiate until you're satisfied with the outcome. Keep doing this until you become an accomplished negotiator in every area.

Major Points

- Your ability to negotiate largely determines how well you do in life.
- The key to negotiating is simply to ask.
- You never know the lowest price until you turn to walk away.
- No urgency, no sale.
- You are free in direct proportion to the number of options that you have developed.
- A negotiating position consists of your essentials, your limits, your maximums, and your minimums.

3

Why You Should Start Your Own Business

Should you start your own business? This is a question that more than 50 percent of adult Americans consider at some time during their careers. More than 70 percent of all men and women coming out of universities with business degrees intend to go out on their own when the time is right.

The answer to this question is a very affirmative *yes*. The very fact that you're thinking about your own business is a good indication that you have the ability to be successful at it. In fact, I've concluded that with very few exceptions, almost anyone has the capacity to start and build a successful business.

We've entered into the age of the entrepreneur in America. More new businesses are being started today than at any other time in history. The U.S. Bureau of the Census reports that over 5 million new businesses were started in 2022. Sweeping changes in every aspect of American life are creating an almost limitless number of new business opportunities for innovative and ambitious men and women. Sharp increases in single parents and women in the paid labor force have created an unrelenting demand for more daycare centers, takeout restaurants, and convenience products. Breakthroughs in science and technology have created entirely new industries. The nation's aging population is triggering a boom in nursing homes, retirement communities, and hospitals. In the years ahead, there will be more opportunities for business success in our society than ever before. As always, the richest rewards will go to those for whom preparation meets opportunity.

Statistics vary, but most say that over two thirds of U.S. millionaires are self-made. I've worked with thousands of these men and women over the years, and they're no different from you and me. Men and women from every age, with every possible limitation of talent, ability, contacts, and marketable skills, have started and built successful businesses and achieved financial independence, and so can you.

Why People Become Entrepreneurs

- Freedom and autonomy
- Economic turbulence
- Reaching a career ceiling
- Having an idea that one's company will not support
- The brother-in-law factor
- Wanting to make money for oneself
- The need to prove that an idea is a good one

Why People Become Entrepreneurs

Let's start off with the reasons why you might leave a salaried position and start off on your own. Those listed below cover perhaps 99 percent of the motivating factors that launch individuals into entrepreneurship.

The number one reason people become entrepreneurs is freedom and autonomy. Most entrepreneurs have a high need to be on their own, be self-responsible, and not answer to anyone else. They need the freedom of setting their own hours and being accountable for the risks and rewards of success.

Many men and women who have a hard time adjusting to a corporate environment are ideally suited to become entrepreneurs. If you have an intense need for personal freedom and autonomy, you may have the individualistic type of mentality that makes you ideal for entrepreneurship.

The second reason why people start businesses is *economic turbulence* in the marketplace. Many talented men and women are finding themselves back on the streets after years of hard work and dedicated service to their corporations. Because of mergers and acquisitions, combined with flattened organizational pyramids, many talented people, especially middle managers, are suddenly finding themselves no longer employed. (By the way, unexpectedly losing a job is a milestone in the life of almost all successful people in America; they have found that being fired or laid off or quitting was the starting point of success.) Often employees receive a lump sum of money—either severance pay, a bonus, or part of their retirement plan—when they leave their job. At this point, they have a choice. They can put the money in the bank and search for new security in another company or start out on their own.

A third reason people start their own businesses is that they realize that they've gone as far as they can go in their current job or industry. They realize that no matter how hard they work, they can't rise much higher by working for someone else. Perhaps the organization's salary and wage structure are fixed. Perhaps the wage structure in the entire industry is such that you can only go so far on someone else's payroll. If this is the case for you, perhaps it's time for you to think of going out and starting your own business.

A fourth reason that people start their own businesses is that they come up with an idea for a new product or process or service that their company is not interested in and will not support. After trying to sell the idea within the company, they decide to prove that their idea is a good one by starting their own business and making it successful. If you see ways of improving your business or industry by increasing revenues, cutting costs, or improving productivity but can't get support for your ideas, this might be a clue that it's time to be on your own.

The fifth reason people start their own business is what I call the *brother-in-law factor.* This is often triggered by seeing a brother-in-law or someone else the person knows who is not particularly talented or intelligent but has started their own business and done extremely well. Often this inspires a person to take the risk of starting a business—just to prove that they are just as good as, if not better than, their brother-in-law.

The sixth reason many people strike out on their own is, they realize that they're working hard making a lot of money for someone else. It dawns on them that they can be making just as much, if not far more, by doing the same things for themselves. At this point, they leave their jobs and start their own businesses.

The seventh reason people take the plunge into entrepreneurship is that they get an idea for a product or service that so excites them that they have to go out and prove that it is a good one. Many individuals come up with ideas that cause them to toss and turn at night, sometimes for weeks and months, until they decide to go out into the marketplace and make those ideas a reality.

The Courage to Begin

Here's the critical part of starting and building your own successful business: *simply having the courage to begin.* Once you start, you learn what you need to know at a rapid rate. When everything you have is at stake—your ego, your money, your reputation, your emotions, your relationships—it's amazing how quickly you learn how to innovate, solve problems, and overcome difficulties. The possibility of losing your shirt is a wonderful stimulation to high performance in entrepreneurship.

Dr. Robert Ronstadt, a professor of business studies, studied successful entrepreneurs for several years. He concluded that one single factor explained the difference between the successful entrepreneurs and the unsuccessful ones who had taken his college courses: the successful entrepreneurs made a start; they stepped out in the face of uncertainty. They dared to go forward and take risks. Those who did not succeed at entrepreneurship almost invariably became victims of paralysis by analysis. They spent an enormous amount of time planning to start a business but never got around to it.

Now here's the important point, which, if you fully understand it, can make you rich. The twelve-year study concluded that when you launch a business, you enter a corridor like a long hallway, the end of which you can't see. As you move down the corridor, you come to doors of opportunity that open for you because you're there. You can't see these doors of opportunity in advance. They only open because you are in motion, because you are moving down the corridor toward your goal of business success. As these doors open, you'll get additional information, ideas, resources, insight, and assistance that will enable you to overcome obstacles, solve problems, and move steadily toward success. The most important thing is to have the courage to plunge into the corridor and begin moving forward.

Be willing to accept feedback and to self-correct. Be willing to learn from every situation, cherish your failures and your mistakes, and extract the valuable lesson from everything that happens to you. By so doing, you continue to move down the corridor, and the doors of opportunity continue to open for you, often in the most unexpected places and in the most unexpected ways.

Qualities of Good Entrepreneurs

In my work with thousands of entrepreneurs, I've never found one who had the courage to begin and the persistence to endure who did not eventually achieve success. Furthermore, almost all entrepreneurs achieve success doing something different from what they'd originally started out doing, but they chop and change and learn and grow. They remain flexible and open to new information, and they keep their eyes on their goal. They don't get bogged down or fall in love with a rigid way of doing things or a specific product or service. Instead, they realize that the entrepreneur's job is to produce and market a product or service at a profit. They're willing to make whatever changes are necessary to achieve this goal.

The first quality that you need is *courage*. The two greatest enemies of humankind are and always have been fear and ignorance. Fear holds us back from taking the actions that would lead to success, while ignorance breeds fear, paralyzing our best intentions. If you don't know what you need to know in order to succeed, it's only logical to be afraid of taking the chance. People often avoid starting

Qualities of Good Entrepreneurs

· Courage
· Optimism and constructive pessimism
· Strategic thinking
· Sales ability
· A strong commitment to winning
· The willingness to work hard

businesses because don't know how and for some reason will not make the effort to learn. This ignorance is manifested in a generalized fear of failure, of the unknown, that paralyzes action and keeps them in their comfort zones, working for wages all the years of their lives.

When you are immersed in ignorance, the risks seem almost insurmountable. Throughout this book, I've been giving you ideas and insights, proven formulas that have worked for millions of men and women, to help you overcome the ignorance that holds most people back. With this new information, you should be able to launch yourself toward the fulfillment of your dreams and aspirations.

The second quality you need is a higher than average level of *optimism*. Successful entrepreneurs tend to have the two qualities of irrepressible optimism and constructive pessimism. Their irrepressible optimism causes them to believe that they will ultimately succeed. Combined with courage, this translates into an attitude of self-confidence that enables them to keep going in the face of adversity. They maintain their courage and optimism through constructive pessimism: they're willing to face reality as it is, to look

at the worst possible thing that can happen as a result of any decision they make. Constructive pessimists are willing to seek out the
opinions of people who may be negative toward their idea. They're
willing to test their ideas by allowing others to poke holes in them.
Constructive pessimists are willing to listen to every reason why
their idea may not work, take it all as information, address the negative feedback, and proceed onward, wiser for the experience.

Entrepreneurs often fail because they become dizzy with positive thinking. They think being happy and cheerful about their idea
is enough to make it a success. They refuse to listen to input from
anyone else. They won't talk to people who may point out the weaknesses in their idea. Surrounding themselves with people who agree
with them, they start down the fatal road to financial failure.

The third quality that you need to succeed as an entrepreneur is
the ability to plan strategically. You need to be able to write out a clear
blueprint of the entire business. This is something that's so important that I'll speak about it in greater detail later.

The fourth quality that you must have to start and build a successful business is that you must be able to *sell.* The ability to sell
the product or service is the absolutely indispensable requirement
for success. If you cannot sell, or if you cannot go into business with
someone else who is excellent at sales, you should put aside the idea
of entrepreneurship for the time being.

But if financial independence is important enough to you, you
can learn how to be an excellent salesperson. During the stage
when they're saving their money and planning their own businesses,
many individuals work for other organizations. There they request
transfers and move around to get a variety of experiences. They
especially insist on getting into the sales force so that they can go
out and call on customers face-to-face. They may not like having to

go out and risk rejection, but they realize that this part of the price they have to pay if they want to start and build a successful business.

If you can sell, you would be crazy not to start your own business.

In fact, if you can sell, you would be crazy not to start your own business. The very fact that you can sell effectively means that you have the key skill that you need to make it a success. By the way, more than 75 percent of the best salespeople in America, both men and women, tend to be categorized as introverts on psychographic tests. They're not particularly outgoing; they're not loud and aggressive. They tend to be very low-keyed, quiet and sensitive to the needs and concerns of their customers. They tend to be very people-oriented. They are not flashy or showy, but they have a wonderful ability to tune in to what another person is saying and listen carefully. Many of these people are among the top 1 percent of salespeople in virtually every business in America.

I mention this fact because many people feel that they don't have the personality to be successful in selling and therefore in entrepreneurship. This is simply not true. More than anything else, you need an intense desire to be on your own and build your own business, as well as the willingness to persist in the face of all difficulties. With those qualities, you can't help but be successful.

Another quality of successful entrepreneurs is that they have strong commitments to *winning*. They are not loud about it, but they're intensely competitive. They have a strong desire to see their product win in the marketplace. In fact, it's a good idea to think of your product or service as capable of becoming the market leader—one of the best in the United States. This attitude is extremely important. Without it, budding entrepreneurs often restrict their vision so much that the product or service never achieves its potential.

Entrepreneurs are tenacious; they're like cats with nine lives: no matter what you throw at them, they keep bouncing back and finding new, better, faster, and easier ways to get the job done. They have tremendous persistence, and once they begin, they never stop short of success.

The final and perhaps most important quality is *the willingness to work hard.* Thousands of self-made millionaires have been interviewed and asked what personal qualities have enabled them to accomplish so much. Almost all of them say that it was plain, old-fashioned hard work. They don't consider themselves to be especially clever or more intelligent than the average, but they all feel that, from an early age on, they were willing to work much harder than the average person.

The average entrepreneurial work week in America is approximately sixty hours. Many entrepreneurs work seventy, eighty, and ninety hours per week. The serious entrepreneur soon casts aside the idea of the five-day work week. You must be prepared to work ten or twelve hours per day, six or seven days per week, for two to four years to make your business a success. A joke says that in order to succeed as an entrepreneur, you only have to work half days, and you can choose whichever twelve-hour period you like.

Now you may not have to work all those hours: you may be lucky, and you may come out with the right product or the right service at the right time, and the market will take off. But you should plan to work these hours. Don't sabotage yourself by working too little during the crucial formative years of your company. If you're prepared to work a high number of hours, it often happens that you don't have to, but if you're not willing to work the hours, failure is almost guaranteed.

Successful entrepreneurship begins with an idea or concept: a vision for a product or service that you can bring to the market and sell at a profit. Successful entrepreneurs are intensely profit-oriented, but also risk-averse. Contrary to the popular myth, they are not risk takers; they are risk avoiders. Entrepreneurs who are risk takers are soon bankrupt. Successful entrepreneurs minimize and reduce risk in the pursuit of profit; they do not increase risk.

Dealing with Murphy's Law

One way to reduce risk is by doing your homework, planning every step of your business in advance, and then staying on top of every important detail. Almost invariably, it is the small, unexpected details that someone assumed would be taken care of that cause you the most problems. To reduce risk, you need to think strategically, plan well in advance, and think through every important detail, making sure that it's covered either by yourself or by someone whom you trust absolutely.

Murphy's Laws

- If anything can possibly go wrong, it will.
- The one thing that will go wrong will be the worst possible thing and at the worst possible time.
- No matter how much time you plan, everything takes longer than you expect.
- Everything always ends up costing you much more than you calculated.
- Nothing is ever done right the first time.

Entrepreneurship is very much subject to Murphy's laws. You've heard the first of them: if anything can possibly go wrong, it will. The corollary to Murphy's first law is that of all the things that can possibly go wrong, the one thing that will go wrong will be the worst possible thing and at the worst possible time.

When I began giving seminars years ago, I learned that the most important tool that a speaker has for communicating with a large audience is his voice and its extension: the sound system. The second most important factor is the lighting system, and the third is the heating and air-conditioning system. Murphy's law applies perfectly to this type of situation. In my experience, the first thing that any speaker has trouble with is the sound system. It packs up; it goes on and off. It creates pockets of silence throughout the room, which cause people to shout and wave their hands, and sometimes it doesn't work at all. The second thing that goes wrong is the lighting. It's either too high or too low or in all the wrong places. And the third thing that goes wrong is the heating and air-conditioning system. In the summer, the furnace will be on, and the room will be 85 degrees. In the winter, the entire system will be malfunctioning, and the room will be 65 degrees. Of course, audiences almost invariably blame the speaker for their discomfort.

Murphy's second law says that no matter how much time you plan, everything takes longer than you expect. The third of Murphy's laws—and this is terribly important for you as an entrepreneur—is that everything always ends up costing you much more than you calculated. The fourth law is that nothing is ever done right the first time.

When you combine these laws, you have a pretty accurate conception of what entrepreneurs have to deal with day after day. The worst possible things that can go wrong—such as the loss of their most important customers or the theft of their cash from their bank account—tend to occur at the worst possible time. No matter how well they plan, they cannot deliver upon their most important promises, because nothing is ever completed on schedule. And no matter how carefully they budget, the product always costs more to make, and they always sell less of it than they projected. And of course, everything takes longer than they imagined.

One of the most important applications of Murphy's law is that no matter how carefully you project to the day when your business will break even, you should take your most conservative estimate and then triple it. If your budget projections indicate that you'll break even and be making a profit six months after starting, in order to be safe and sane, you should triple that six-month estimate to eighteen months. Thousands of business cases have proved that tripling is far more likely to be accurate than your best guess based on your financial projections.

The Business Plan

Once you have a vision or a concept, you need to prepare a business plan. A business plan is the blueprint for your enterprise. Your ability to analyze and assemble all of the information necessary to create an accurate business plan is one of the most important tests of whether or not you'll succeed. Creating a business plan—whether it takes you two weeks, two months, or two years—is essential to getting the money you need to set up your business in the proper way. The business plan is like your Bible. It is so important that I'll give you all the elements of it later.

Ways to Go into Business

There are basically three ways of getting into business. You can start it from scratch, you can buy an existing business, or you can purchase a franchise from the thousands of companies that sell franchise operations. One source says there were some 790,500 franchise organizations in operation in the United States in 2022. The leading franchisers are familiar companies such as Chick-fil-A, the UPS Store, Ace Hardware, and McDonald's.

To start a business, it is usually essential to have some capital accumulated. It is vital to save at least 10 percent of your income to take advantage of an opportunity when it comes along. One of the most priceless of all opportunities is a great business idea or concept. If you set aside 10 percent of your income, you will have money available when your chance comes.

Let's say that you have no money, but you're willing to take a chance, work hard, start off in the face of uncertainty, set goals, plan strategically, and even put together a business plan. What do you do then?

You can do one of two things. First, you can take a sales job in a field where you'd like to start your own business. You can go to work and learn on the job. A gentleman who went through one of my seminars followed my advice to the letter. He began managing his time very carefully. Within two months, had doubled his sales output and his sales income. He began saving 10 percent of his income, and within a year he was saving almost 30 percent. He set out clear, specific goals for his life and looked around him to see which business he could go into. He decided to go into a business in computer services and immediately selected the best company in that field in his area. He got a job selling for that company so that he could earn while he learned. He has a game plan now, which will have him financially capable of starting his own successful business within three years. Do you think he'll achieve it? His chances are extremely good.

The first thing to do is work in your chosen field and become knowledgeable and experienced. You've heard it said that 80 percent of new businesses fail within the first five years. The fact is that 99 percent of businesses started by people *with no business experience* fail within the first two years. However, more than 90 percent of businesses started by people with previous business experience, especially in the same field, go on to succeed in the marketplace.

More than 90 percent of businesses started by people with previous business experience, especially in the same field, go on to succeed in the marketplace.

It is extremely important to learn what you need to know in order to be successful. It's far smarter to work for two or three or five years with a successful, progressive company, taking all the training you can get, saving your money, and learning everything you possibly can, before you start your own business. This will save you many thousands of dollars and years of hard work learning on your own.

Multilevel Marketing

If you lack experience and money, another approach to entrepreneurship is multilevel or network marketing. Many fortunes have been started by individuals who got their initial experience and capital by selling multilevel marketing (MLM) products. In the United States today there are thousands of companies selling every conceivable product in this way. Among the biggest and best-known are Amway, Avon, Herbalife, and Tupperware. It's one of the fastest-growing methods for the distribution of products and services, and you can get into a multilevel marketing organization with very little money.

To succeed in multilevel marketing, you must be prepared to work very hard. You must be prepared to work evenings and weekends, a minimum of ten to twenty extra hours per week in addition to your full-time job. If you're willing to do this, MLM could be your starting point toward financial independence. Here are my recommendations on what you should look for in a bona fide first-class multilevel network marketing company.

First of all, the company must have high-quality products with a good reputation in the marketplace. The products should do what they're sold to do. Avoid medium- or low-quality products at all costs.

The second thing to look for in a multilevel marketing company is fair prices. Many MLM products are outrageously priced compared to what else is available in the marketplace. Look at the prices of competitive products, and evaluate the differences objectively.

The third thing to look for is a 100 percent unconditional money back guarantee for each and every product that you or anybody else buys from this company. If people aren't completely satisfied, they should be able to return even the empty containers and get their money back. If you are not completely satisfied, you should be able to turn in your extra products and get your money back as well.

The fourth thing to look for is minimum requirements for inventory. You shouldn't have to put up much money upfront. The beauty of a good multilevel marketing company is that you can sell the product or service from samples or brochures and only buy the product for resale when you've taken an order from your customer. Any company that requires you to keep a large stock of inventory is probably planning to make all their money from you rather than from retail sales of the product.

A good MLM organization should have prompt delivery and efficient internal accounting. They should be able to give you accurate statements, and you should be able to get the products that you need for resale in a timely manner.

The better multilevel marketing companies also have strong support organizations. For you, this is absolutely indispensable. You need all the training, product knowledge, motivation, and personal development you can get. Many people work with a multilevel marketing firm for a few years and go on to build their businesses in totally separate fields, but what they learn with an MLM organization is invaluable to them in building up any other business. You need to have people that you can meet, work with, talk to, and learn from on a regular basis, and that's what a multilevel marketing organization should give you.

Be sure to look for honesty and integrity in the parent company. One of the most important assets that any company has is its reputation. It's an exercise in frustration to try to sell a product when the parent company has a bad reputation because of a lawsuit or failure to fulfill its past commitments.

The final thing that you should look in a multilevel marketing company is that the product should be consumable. Once you've created a customer, that customer should use up the products and like them so much that they will come back to you to reorder over and over. This is not only the basis for a successful multilevel marketing business, it's the basis for a successful business of just about any kind.

For little or no investment, you can start a part-time business as a multilevel marketer, selling to your friends and relatives at first, and then building up a broader customer base. Many enterprising men and women have built substantial second incomes and even achieved financial independence with MLM organizations. So if you have little money but lots of time, this could be a good place for you to start.

Your Dream Business

Now here's an exercise for you. What sort of business have you always wanted to get into? What products or services do you most enjoy using? What type of economic activity attracts your attention and holds your interest? What things do you do in your spare time that could be turned into a business? What unique talents and abilities do you have that could lead you in the direction of a business that would be ideal for you? What products or services could you get excited about selling? Which businesspeople do you particularly admire? What entrepreneurs have you read about that you've wanted to emulate? If you could pick one businessperson you know, directly or indirectly, whom would you most want to be like? What qualities does this person have that you would like to have?

By looking deeply into yourself, into your own interests and abilities, you'll often get the germ of the concept that could lead to starting your own business and building your own fortune.

A Special Talent to Market

Anyone who really wants to can start and build a successful business in America today. We know this is true because just about every kind of person who ever existed has already started and built a successful business and gotten rich as a result. There are twelve- and thirteen-year-old children who started businesses in junior high school and become wealthy by the early twenties. There are sixty-five- and seventy-year-old men and women who have started successful businesses. Individuals from every walk of life, with every conceivable limitation and obstacle, have accepted the challenge of entrepreneurship and succeeded at it, and so can you.

How to Find Business Ideas

The following material is designed to suggest some of the things you can do, starting right now, to begin growing your own business. If you act on what you learn below, you may be in business yourself before the end of the week.

The purpose of a business is not to make a profit; it is to create and keep customers. Making a profit is the result of creating and keeping your customers in a cost-effective way. All successful businesses focus intently on what the customer wants and how to satisfy the customer. Successful entrepreneurs see themselves as working for and on behalf of their customers, and they look at everything through the eyes of their customers; this enables them to satisfy their customers better than their competitors.

Because of rapid changes in technology, 80 percent of the most popular products and services that will be used five years from today don't even exist right now. They have yet to be developed and brought into the market, making fortunes for the ambitious entrepreneurs who have seen their possibilities before anyone else.

Begin with yourself. Look into your own talents and abilities. You may have a million-dollar idea in your own mind. Look back at your experience and your background. What have you learned that could be turned into a business? Examine your knowledge, the things that you've studied and learned over the years. Is there an idea or a possibility for a new business in your existing knowledge bank? What are your interests? You'll tend to be most successful in a business area that interests you, that holds your attention—something in which you can become completely absorbed. Successful people lose themselves in their work, and this is only possible if you really care about the product or service that you're bringing to the marketplace.

Look carefully at your current job. What part of your work do you do especially well? Look at your position in your business. Is there something there that suggests what you might be able to do in a business of your own? Your best opportunities probably lie right under your feet, right within your own work and your own knowledge and interests. See if there isn't the germ of an excellent business idea just waiting for you to reach out and touch it. Look for a product or service about which you can become enthusiastic. You'll always be most successful doing something you really love. Every product or service must have a champion: someone who absolutely believes in the value and importance of the product to others.

Look for an improvement on an existing product or service rather than for something brand-new. Look for something that's at the same level of quality or of better quality at the same price. Look for some way to add additional features or functions to a product that people are already using. An idea only needs to be 10 percent new or better to capture a substantial market share.

In fact, you're much better off going into an established field than starting a new product or service. More than 80 percent of all new products fail in the first year, even when they're developed by the most successful companies in America. It's foolish to think that you can come into the marketplace with something that no one else has ever thought of—much less something that no customer has ever bought—and be successful against all the odds. Most self-made millionaires achieve their wealth in established fields, selling established products to establish customers, just doing them better.

When looking for an idea, don't look for easy money; don't look for gimmicks or knickknacks that have no practical purpose or value. Don't listen to get-rich-quick schemes, which suggest that you can make a lot of money in a short time through no real effort or investment of your own. Don't look for rewards without working. Anyone who suggests a business opportunity whereby you can make a lot of money without a sustained period of hard work is probably proposing a waste of time and money.

Another place to look for new products and services is in newspaper stories, magazine articles, advertisements in a variety of publications, and of course online. You can read trade periodicals that are aimed at people in your industry. Whenever someone has an idea for a new product or service, they immediately begin to advertise it in publications that are read by people in those fields. You may read *Popular Mechanics*, *Success* magazine, *Inc.*, or various computer magazines, both in print and online, to find new products or services. You may be able to get the right to distribute these products or services in your area. These articles or advertisements may also give you ideas for developing new products or services of your own to serve these markets. In addition to Internet sources, your local library usually has a great selection of magazines. If you spend an afternoon going through publications in your library, reading the advertisements carefully and taking down names and addresses to send away for information, you may be able to find the idea that you can use to launch your business.

Another way to find ideas for new products especially is to go to trade shows. An estimated 13,000 trade shows take place annually throughout the United States. All you need to get into a trade show is a business card and perhaps a small registration fee. Tell them that you're a retail customer and you're coming to look at the products and services. Sometimes you'll see new products that have just come on the market; if you can get the rights to sell them in your city, they can form the foundation of your new business.

You should also tell your friends that you're starting your own business and ask them to keep an eye open for products and services that you might offer. You'll be amazed at the amount of information that your friends are exposed to on a day-to-day basis. They'll often introduce you to people who have ideas that you can use.

Look into your own field or skills. You may have a million-dollar idea in your own mind. It's been said that the average person, driving to and from work each year, has four ideas, any one of which could make them a millionaire. Catch the idea and write it down. Carry around a small pad with you all the time; whenever you think of an idea that could help you launch or build a business, write it down quickly before you lose it. Many fortunes have been built on this simple technique for capturing useful ideas.

Keep alert to new business opportunities around you. Develop a moneymaking attitude. Put yourself in the mind of a customer, and when you see a new business concept, ask yourself, is that the kind of product or service that people will buy and use? If it is, you may be able to imitate or improve on it. When you see products sold in other places, you can acquire the rights to sell them in your market area. Often a letter to a manufacturer or distributor will give you the right to sell that product or service in your vicinity.

One final point: you'll only be successful marketing and selling something that you believe in, would use yourself, and would recommend to your best friend. People often approach me with ideas for products that they themselves would never think of using. They believe that even though they don't like the item themselves, someone else will be willing to pay them good money for it. This is simply silly.

Research and Testing Your Idea

Let's say you've found a product or service idea. How do you determine whether it's a good idea? How do you test it before investing too much time or money in it?

Market research and testing are essential to the success of a new product.

You must do some fast, cheap market research. Before embarking on any new business venture, you must spend considerable time in research. Your payoff will be in excess of ten to one in the amount of time and money you'll save or earn as the result of your investment in this research. Its purpose is to find out every detail of the product or business. Study it carefully so that you know it intimately. Nobody should be able to ask you a single question about your idea without your having a clear, intelligent answer. Further suggestions:

1. Read trade magazines, articles, and stories on the business, the industry, or the occupation. Go to the library to the periodical index and do your homework. Find out everything that's been written in the area you're thinking about. This research process may take two weeks, two months, or two years, but you must do it before you finally decide that this is the business for you.

2. Seek out people in the same business and ask their opinion. If you're thinking of starting a dry-cleaning establishment, going into a multilevel marketing business, buying a franchise, or start-

ing a business service, speak to other people who are doing the same thing and ask them for their advice. Often young entrepreneurs refuse to speak to anyone else for fear that someone else will steal their idea. But there are very few original ideas in any business or industry; most of them have been thought of a hundred or a thousand times. What has been lacking is the intelligence, creativity, and drive to put them into action.

3. Ask your bank for advice. If you don't have a bank account, open one at the largest commercial branch in your area, and ask to speak to one of their commercial lending officers. Tell them you're thinking of starting a new business in this area and ask for their advice. Banks have an enormous amount of valuable information available to them, including personal experiences with many other businesses like yours. Often a banker will ask you a few questions and give you insights that will save you a fortune in time and money.

4. Ask your friends, family, and acquaintances for information and ideas. Ask everyone you know if they have any knowledge of the business that you're considering.

5. Visit prospective customers and ask if they would buy your product or service. If it's going to be sold at retail, ask a retailer if they could sell it. One of the best ways to find out if your product or service is any good is to go to the kind of person who you think is eventually going to buy the product or service and see what they think of it. This is not a perfect test, but you absolutely must do it before producing or import the product in any quantity.

6. Research all competitors for the product or service, and ask yourself this key question: why would someone switch to buy from me? Why would someone stop using an existing supplier of the product or service and start using me, a completely unknown

quantity? If you can't answer this question with a very good reason, it could be that your business or service idea is not well thought out.

7. When considering a business that is for sale, find out why. Very few people will sell a successful business.

8. Look at the business that you're thinking of starting or buying as though you are going to be in it for twenty years. Develop a long-term perspective. When you think of being in a business for twenty years, you tend to be far more careful about your decisions than if you think you're going to get in and out of it quickly. The long-term perspective sharpens the short-term perspective and makes you more astute at making the decisions that will affect the future of your enterprise.

9. Seek out and listen carefully to people who are negative towards your idea. Negative viewpoints can be invaluable to you and save you a fortune in time and money. Very often other people will be able to point out a flaw in your thinking that you haven't seen—a flaw that would in itself be enough to cause your business venture to fail if you weren't able to correct it.

Test Marketing

Once you've settled on the product or service and done some quick market research to assure yourself that this is a good idea, here are some ideas on how you can test-market before you launch your business.

1. Make a prototype or create or get a sample of the product so that you can show or at least photograph it.

2. Before you can start your business, you need accurate prices and delivery dates from suppliers. You need to know exactly how

much to charge for your product, and how much it's going to cost you to produce in the first place.

3. Get a buyer's personal opinion. Approach a prospective customer and ask whether they would buy it and what price they would pay. Call on individuals who make buying decisions. Only a professional buyer can give you an accurate insight into whether or not you have a winner. If you're going to offer your products for sale at retail, try a one-store test offer by putting the product into the store on consignment.

Often you can do a test with a single customer. Go to a single customer and ask if they would buy or use the product or service. This can give you valuable feedback that will help you make the right decisions later.

4. Show your product at trade shows attended by professional buyers. They will give you rapid feedback and tell you whether or not you have a product that's going to sell well.

5. Ask your friends and relatives (and even yourself) if you or they would buy or use the product or service. Sometimes your family and friends can give you good feedback and point out holes in your idea. They are not the beginning and end of your decision-making process, but they can be very helpful.

The Business Plan

If you've done your homework, you're ready to begin putting together your business plan. The development of a complete business plan before beginning operations is one of the most important things you ever do as an entrepreneur. In fact, your ability to create a business plan is a measure of whether or not you are cut out to succeed in the first place.

Your business plan becomes the blueprint that you will use to build your business from the ground up. It's the plan that you will follow day by day, dollar by dollar. One primary reason for success is the development of this accurate, detailed business plan in advance, and one primary reason for failure—especially in entrepreneurship—is the unwillingness or inability to put together a complete business plan before beginning.

A business plan requires an enormous amount of time and energy. You may have to research for many weeks to get all the information that you require to complete it in such a form that it will serve as the proper framework to guide your decision-making.

Eight Parts of a Business Plan

Many books are available on business plan writing, and there are several inexpensive software programs that you can purchase for this purpose as well. I'll just briefly touch on the eight key parts of the business plan so that you have an idea of the information that you'll require.

1. THE CONCEPT

Part one of the business plan is a description of the concept or idea. You outline the purpose of the company: why it is being created in the first place. A company is merely a bundle of resources brought together to enter the marketplace and satisfy an as yet unmet customer need or solve an as yet unsolved customer problem. In your description of the concept, you address why the business is being brought into existence and what opportunity is not currently being met.

2. THE BUSINESS OBJECTIVE

Part two outlines the business objective, describing how much you intend to sell over the next two to five years. What market share do you hope to gain? How much profit do you intend to generate?

3. MARKET ANALYSIS

The third part of the business plan is the market analysis. Here you describe the research and investigation that led you to the development of the concept. You clearly discuss the entire marketplace and specific customers. You describe how the product will get to the market, how it will be sold, and how it will be advertised and promoted. You describe the competitors, both existing and in future, and how and why your product or service is superior to theirs. You outline how the product will be priced and why you can charge these prices. You set out the history of similar products and services in the marketplace—what they're now doing or what has happened to them and the reasons for it. You show how many of your products or how many of your services you'll have to sell to break even and make a profit based on the best projections that you've been able to develop.

The key to performing this market analysis—which lies at the heart of a successful business plan—is asking the right questions. Some important questions that you can ask in marketing are the following:

1. Who exactly is your customer? Describe a typical customer for your product or service in complete detail, including everything about them that will make them trade money for your offering. What are your customer's age, income, occupation, education, interests, and background?

Eight Parts of a Business Plan

1. Concept
2. Business objective
3. Market analysis
4. Production facilities
5. Advertising and selling
6. Organizational structure
7. Financial projections
8. Ownership structure

The second question is, where are your customers? Where are they concentrated? Are they local, nationwide, or worldwide? However you describe your customers, you will have to explain how you're going to market, sell, and deliver to them.

2. How does your customer normally purchase your product? Through what marketing channels? Does your customer purchase your product as the result of direct selling, in stores, by direct mail? Knowing how your customer is accustomed to buying your product is an important part of your business plan, and especially your marketing plan.

3. Here's the key question: why will your customer purchase your product? What specific benefit will your customer get from it? What problems will it solve? The answer to the question *why* is one of the most important ones in market research. Answering it incorrectly is the primary reason businesses fail.

The answer to the question *why* is one of the most important ones in market research.

Another question to ask in marketing is, who is your competition? Who is currently selling to your customer? What is your competition? What is causing your customer *not* to buy your product or service at this time? Your competition could be a company offering a competitive product, or even an idea or mindset that holds the customer back from buying at this time.

Here's another question in marketing: why do your customers buy from your competition? What benefits do they think they receive from your competitor? What's most attractive about your competitor's product? Furthermore, how are you going to offset the perceived benefits and advantages of buying from your competitor in your customer's mind? Why would or should they switch from your competition to buy from you? What is especially attractive about your product or service that makes it different?

Here's the key to all business successes: *your area of excellence.* In strategic planning, it's called your *competitive advantage.* In marketing, we call it your *unique selling proposition.* It is the aspect of your product or service that makes it superior in some way to any similar product or service in the marketplace. All successful businesses in America are based on the development and maintenance of meaningful competitive advantage. The company analyzes its customers carefully and produces a product that satisfies them better than any competitive product in that price and quality range. Sometimes competitive advantage can be achieved by simply having your business located closer to customers, such as a corner grocery store or a 7-Eleven. Sometimes competitive advantage means that you are a low-cost supplier for products or services that are consumed in large quantities. The tremendous success of Walmart is based on their being an everyday low-price supplier of a wide range of products for the middle-class American family.

What is your area of excellence? What about your product or service makes it superior to other choices? Customers are not interested in your success or failure; they are only interested in themselves; they're perfectly selfish. They will only buy what they feel is the best product or service that they can get at this time, at this quality, for this amount of money.

Before you can start your own business with any hope of success, you must be able to describe your competitive advantage in twenty-five words or less. This becomes the primary reason you're going into business in the first place, as well as the central focus of your advertising and promotion. Your ability to achieve this advantage and hold it against competitors will determine whether and how fast you become successful.

FOUR KEYS TO SUCCESS IN MARKETING

It's said that there are four keys to success in marketing. The first is *specialization* or doing something in an excellent fashion. All successful businesses specialize in a narrow area and do one or a few things very well. They achieve excellence in a specific product or service area.

The second key to marketing success is *differentiation*: the way you make your product or service stand out in the mind of your customer. You make it appear different as the result of your competitive advantage or your advertising. This is often called your *area of uniqueness.* If your product or service is not unique in some way, it will seldom achieve worthwhile market share or lasting profitability.

Four Keys in Marketing

1. Specialization
2. Differentiation
3. Segmentation
4. Concentration

The third key to marketing strategy is *segmentation.* You segment your market when you identify the customers for whom your competitive advantage is the most beneficial. Your ability to identify your market segment will determine how much of your product you sell, how fast you sell it, and how much profit you'll earn.

The fourth key to marketing strategy is *concentration.* This means that once you've decided upon your ideal customers and market segment, you'll concentrate all of your resources single-mindedly on selling most of your product or service to this specific customer group.

These four keys—specialization, differentiation, segmentation, and concentration—are all essential to a successful marketing strategy.

The Four P's of Marketing

Another area that you must cover in part three, the market analysis section of your business plan is the marketing mix. The marketing mix is also made up of four ingredients: the four P'S.

The first P in the marketing mix is *product*: exactly what product or service are you going to sell to this specific market?

The second P is *price.* How are you going to price the product? Are you going to mark it up by a certain amount based on your actual cost? Are you going to add a specific percentage to it? Are you going to attempt to cream the market by charging premium

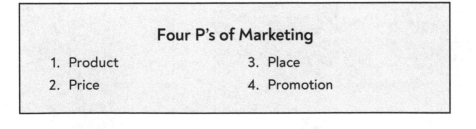

Four P's of Marketing

1. Product	3. Place
2. Price	4. Promotion

prices? Are you going to maximize the market share by charging discounted prices? What sort of prices are you going to give for quantity purchases? How will you price it at both wholesale and retail? Thinking through the pricing of a product for a specific market is very, very important.

The third P in the marketing mix is *place*: where are you going to sell this product? What geographical location, in what kind of stores, or over what market area are you going to sell it?

The fourth P is *promotion*. How are you going to advertise and promote this product at this price, at this place, to this customer? How will you advertise, and how much will you spend on it? How are you going to tell the marketplace about your product or service? How are you going to inform customers that this product or service is available at this price, at this place? Your advertising and promotion strategy is vital to the success of your whole plan.

4. PRODUCTION FACILITIES

Section four of your business plan covers the production facilities necessary to create the product or service. If you're going to manufacture something, in this part of the plan you would explain your requirements for equipment, facilities, building, raw materials, labor, and other supplies and resources. You would spell them out in terms of both quantities required and the prices that you'll have to pay for them.

In addition to production, you would describe the quality controls you would install as well as the product's packaging and transportation requirements. You produce a program for the initial time period and a schedule that outlines who is to do what and by when. You develop a budget and clearly spell out what quantitative and qualitative results you expect in getting ready to produce the product or service.

5. ADVERTISING AND SELLING

Section five of your business plan covers all of the elements of marketing that we've discussed, plus a few more. In this section, you explain how you're going to advertise and sell the product. You explain the features and benefits that you would emphasize in your promotions. You lay out a program and schedule for your initial promotional period as well as the budget for spending and how much in sales you expect to result from this expenditure.

6. ORGANIZATIONAL STRUCTURE

Section six is the organizational structure of your new company: the people who will be expected to carry out the business plan. You describe who would be accountable for what, and to whom. Who would be the boss, and who would be the employee? What experience and background would they have? How would you staff your company in the initial time period, and what schedule would you use for staffing? What would be your budget for bringing together the human resources that you require? What results would you expect, and within what time period, from hiring, training, and deploying the people?

7. FINANCIAL PROJECTIONS

Part seven brings together all the numbers you have developed in the earlier parts of the plan. This part is your fund flow and financial projections. You describe your projected cash flow from operations. You spell out exactly what kind of money you expect to bring in, what kind of money would flow out, and how that money would be spent. You develop a *pro forma profit and loss statement.* In this statement, you calculate, by your very best estimate, the amount that you plan to sell each month for the first eighteen to twenty-four months after you start. From that monthly figure, you would deduct all of the expenses that you would incur to achieve those sales. At the end of this column, you would come out with a profit or loss figure for each month.

Most businesses will be in a loss position for the first three, six, nine, or even twelve months. Some businesses lose money for two or three years. In any case, your ability to accurately project your cash flow requirements is considered by many experts to be the acid test of successful entrepreneurship. For bankers and venture capital suppliers, your ability to make your numbers tells them whether you are competent or incompetent. You then produce pro forma balance sheets showing where you would be at the end of each quarter and at the end of each year.

Finally, as part of your financial projections, you would show your program for monitoring and controlling the funds as well as the people and systems that will be included in the financial planning and financial controls.

8. OWNERSHIP STRUCTURE

Part eight of your business plan, the final part, describes the ownership structure. This includes all the money that you'll require, the form of business that you'll select, and how the ownership of the company is going to be divided up in terms of equity and debt.

If you're starting your own business, the best legal form is a *sole proprietorship*. You can start a sole proprietorship today by simply deciding that you are one. It's that simple. If you start the business with your own name, you don't even need to register. You can open a bank account, print business cards and stationery, publish advertising brochures, rent offices, go into the marketplace, and begin to sell. A sole proprietorship has one specific benefit: any losses that you incur while running it can be deducted from all of your other sources of income in that year.

By contrast, if you set up a corporation, which many entrepreneurs rush to do, only those losses that can be offset by profits in the corporation can be deducted for tax purposes. Some people think that they can limit their legal liability by forming a corporation. The fact is that when your business is young, you will have to sign personal guarantees for virtually every penny you borrow from virtually every single source. A corporate structure doesn't protect you at all, because the lenders and suppliers have direct recourse to you and all of your assets, usually for all time.

I recommend that you start off as a sole proprietorship and register the name of your new company so that no one else can start a company with the same name. When your company becomes profitable, you can incorporate. The best way to incorporate is as an S corporation. An S corporation is structured so that there are no taxes paid on its income at source; rather, all the profits flow through to the owner or owners of the company on their personal income tax statements. I believe that if the company is going to have fewer than thirty-five shareholders, it is best structured as an S corporation to avoid the double taxation of profits (at both the corporate and individual levels).

* * *

The wonderful thing about America is that you can go into business today simply by deciding that you are now a business and you are operating. You may not have bought or sold anything yet, but that will come soon enough. You can be an entrepreneur just by saying that that is what you are. The design of this business plan as I've just described it is vital to the success of your enterprise.

Seven Simple Formulas for Success

Now here are seven simple formulas for business success.

1. Set a specific goal for yourself and begin to visualize it as a reality. Write it and rewrite it over and over again. If it's a financial goal, keep that number fixed in your mind day and night until you begin to attract into your life people and circumstances that make that goal a reality.

2. Look for a problem that you can solve with a product or service that is of both high quality and good value. The most successful and profitable businesses are based on selling high-quality products at good prices. People will always pay more for a better-quality product, and you'll eventually end up earning more and being prouder of what you're doing than if you sell a medium- or poor-quality product at lower discount prices.

3. Be willing to start small and learn your business thoroughly. Take the time to thoroughly understand every detail of what you're doing before you move ahead.

4. Test every major move before you invest in it. One key to success in business, especially in marketing, is to test, test, test. Never

---

Seven Formulas for Success

1. Set a specific goal.
2. Look for a problem you can solve.
3. Be willing to start small.
4. Test every major move before investing.
5. Expand on the basis of your successes.
6. Choose personnel carefully.
7. Use OPM: other people's money.

---

plunge ahead with a full commitment until you've tested the product, service, and method of advertising, and you've sufficiently demonstrated that it will work on a larger scale.

5. Expand your business on the basis of your successes, out of your profits, one step at a time. Don't be in a hurry to grow rapidly. Ninety-five percent of small businesses in the United States have fewer than twenty employees. The average small business that has been in operation for ten years in this country has only four employees. Many of the most successful businesses took five to ten years to lay down the foundation for rapid growth before they took off. Be willing to do the same yourself if necessary.

6. Carefully select the people you will need to help you expand. The smartest thing you can do is hire the right people and pay them well. The biggest problems that you'll ever have in business will be from people that you hire quickly without enough thought. Be very careful concerning anybody that you are going to bring in as part of your business.

7. Use financial leverage, or OPM: other people's money. Use your business, borrowing based on your cash flow from your business, to leverage yourself into even greater profitability and a bigger business. The most important thing that you get from owning your own business is steady cash flow that you can use to build up your personal estate.

Many businesspeople achieve their greatest successes in unexpected areas. They begin a business but find it isn't as profitable as they had anticipated, so they change direction, using their experience and momentum, and strike pay dirt in something else. Act, move forward, one step at a time, learning and growing as you go. There's enough information available in virtually every field for you to become knowledgeable enough to achieve success, but action is necessary.

An Action Exercise

Now here's an exercise for you. Take out a pad of paper and make a list of every job that you've ever had and every job within each job that you've ever done. Write these all down as fast as you can.

Now, on a separate list, write down all the talents, skills, abilities, and special knowledge that you have in any area. Write down all the things that you've learned as the result of your study and work experience. Write them all down as quickly as you can.

On the basis of these two lists, write down a minimum of twenty different businesses you can think of that you might be suited to go into; write down fifty ideas if you can. If you need examples, you can search the Internet to stimulate your thinking.

Now compare the three lists and ask yourself this question: based on the work that I've done in the past and the knowledge and experience that I've gained, in what business field do I think I could be the most successful?

If you feel you could be successful in more than one, set priorities and determine which one you think you'd enjoy the most. Which one would you enjoy the second most? Which one would you enjoy the third most?

Set a goal and make a plan to acquire information about the business that seems to be the most likely one for you. Begin doing your research online. Ask people about the business. Look for some way of improving the business and making it more attractive to a customer or more profitable for the operators. Sometimes you'll come up with an idea or insight that nobody else sees—one that can be the basis for your business fortune—but you must begin, and begin today.

Major Points

- Almost anyone has the capacity to start and build a successful business.
- The critical part of starting your business: having the courage to begin.
- Successful entrepreneurship begins with a vision for a product or service that you can bring to the market and sell at a profit.
- There are three ways of getting into business: starting it from scratch, buying an existing business, or purchasing a franchise.
- One of the most important assets that any company has is its reputation.
- The fundamental purpose of a business is to create and keep customers.
- You'll only be successful selling something that you believe in.
- You must do market research before releasing a product.
- The key to business success is your competitive advantage or unique selling proposition.
- A business plan is essential for any startup.

4

How to Get Startup Capital

Theodore Roosevelt once said, "Do what you can with what you have right where you are." You have the ability to start your own business right now, right where you are, in your current situation, no matter what it is.

The most important quality for success as an entrepreneur is an intense burning desire to be in a business of your own. If you back your desire with drive, ambition, and self-discipline to do what you should do when you should do it, whether you feel like it or not, you'll be on your way. These qualities of character are far more important than the temporary advantages of money.

Most people who dream of starting their own businesses complain that they don't have the money. When I was growing up and right into my thirties, I had a dream of financial independence, but I never seemed to have enough money even to pay my bills. As I looked around me, I found that most people were in more or less the same situation: they spend everything they make and a little more besides. Even if a good business opportunity did come along, they wouldn't be able to take advantage of it. This is why I have emphasized the importance of beginning to save 10 percent of your net income. This is the measure of how much desire, drive, and discipline you really have. The world is full of people who are wishing and hoping but not doing anything about it. Only when you are willing to sacrifice in the short term to be prepared for opportunity in the long term will you begin to make any progress.

In this chapter, I'm going to give you a variety of ways to get the money you need to start the business that you want to start. Most of the greatest fortunes in America were started on a shoestring. Andrew Carnegie, who built U.S. Steel and became one of the nation's richest men, began as a Scottish immigrant with only 75 cents in his pocket. John D. Rockefeller, who became the world's richest man, began as a clerk earning $3.75 a week. Many men and women, starting at menial jobs, pulled themselves up through their own efforts to achieve great wealth. It's not the amount of money that you start with, but the amount of ambition and determination that you have, that will determine your success.

Sweat Equity

The most important investment you can make in your new business is *sweat equity*: your investment of time and hard work. It may take ten, twelve, or fourteen hours a day, seven days per week, for months or even years. But you can translate this sweat equity into real wealth if you stay at it long enough.

I've already covered the starting points of your new business. First is the idea or concept: something that you really want to sell, that you really want people to take advantage of. The second step is the preparation of a detailed business plan. Please do not underestimate the importance of this document. Don't be in too much of a hurry. Take your time. As an ancient adage says, make haste slowly. Take enough time to do your homework and learn all the details of the business you're interested in.

Once you have your business plan, you'll have a pretty good idea of how much money you need to get started. Even if you have no money at all, there are several things you can do to get the capital you need.

Bootstrapping

The best way to build your business is through *bootstrapping*. With bootstrapping, you start small and invest your time rather than your money or someone else's. You work hard to sell your product and then plow all of your profits back into the business. You grow the business out of positive cash flow. You pull yourself up through your own hard work rather than through raising capital from outside sources.

Businesses built on bootstrapping sometimes grow more slowly than ones with ample financial resources. But there's a distinct advantage to bootstrapping that other businesses don't have: when you're pulling yourself up hour by hour and dollar by dollar, you tend to be smarter and learn faster. And if you have little money instead of a cushion of cash to fall back on, you become far more creative in generating sales and keeping your costs under control than you would if you felt you could absorb a few mistakes.

As we've already seen, one of the best ways to bootstrap yourself into business is by becoming a multilevel or network marketer. You can get into an MLM business with very little money out of your pocket. All you should have to buy is a sample kit and some basic manuals. From then on, you can make sales from your samples, collect the money, pick up the product, and deliver it to your customer. Many fortunes are being made in MLM by men and women who started with no money. By virtue of their hard work, they were able to pull themselves up by their own bootstraps into financial independence.

Many people think that they're too good—too well educated or too intelligent—to sell multilevel marketing products. Yet I know many people who barely have high school diplomas yet are making tens of thousands of dollars per month by working hard in multilevel marketing businesses. Many doctors, dentists, architects, engineers, and lawyers are leaving their professions and going into MLM because they see tremendous opportunities to start and build a self-perpetuating money machine.

Successful entrepreneurs are never afraid to do dog work. They're never afraid to roll up their sleeves and do the hard, dirty work that's necessary to get any business off the ground. They're willing to sweep floors, load boxes, and make midnight deliveries if that's what it takes.

Successful entrepreneurs are never afraid to do dog work.

Enough Money to Start

To start your own business, you only have to have enough money to get started. You don't need enough to compete with General Motors or IBM. You just need to create a reasonable, conservative business plan and gather sufficient capital to launch your enterprise.

One of the primary ways that entrepreneurs begin is with savings or the sale of personal assets. Thousands of successful businesses have been started by individuals who sold or mortgaged their homes, sold their boats and personal possessions, and even liquidated everything they had in order to get the cash to start. You may have life insurance with a cash surrender value that you can turn in or borrow against. You may have savings bonds put aside for a rainy day. You may have assets around the house that you can sell for the cash that you need to get started.

It's good exercise to make a list of every single thing that you own and go over it to decide which of them are worth giving up in exchange for your business. Everything requires sacrifice, and starting your own business will often require the greatest sacrifices of your life.

Many successful businesses have been started and built on credit cards and cash advances. I've met many people who started and built their businesses by using their credit cards, and I've had to survive on cash advances from credit cards myself on at least two occasions.

The third source of money that's available to you is to borrow against something you own. Often a bank will lend you money against your car if it's almost paid off. You can borrow against your furniture, your boat, or any other large possession that you own. Many entrepreneurs borrow to the hilt against their homes to get the cash they need to get started.

Another major resource is *love money*: money that people give to you because they love you. Love money comes from your parents, your relatives, your brothers and sisters, and your friends. Perhaps 99 percent of new businesses in America are started on personal savings and love money, because this is the only place that you're going to be able to raise money without a successful business track record or assets to sell or borrow against.

Often your business associates and the contacts that you have developed during the course of your career will take a chance on you by investing in your business. When I've borrowed love money from my friends and relatives at various times, I've personally guaranteed each loan and paid them an above-market rate of interest, such as 20 percent, for the life of the loan.

Sometimes your friends and relatives will want you to sell them a share of your business. This is not a good idea, but if you do, write out an agreement with a sliding scale of share prices that enables you to buy them out at a profit if the business is successful.

Don't Take Partners

Here's another important rule: don't take partners. In the previous chapter, I recommended either a sole proprietorship or a corporation as the legal structure for your business. I said nothing about partnerships—and for a good reason. Partnerships are the worst kind of business arrangement. They have such a high failure rate that you can be almost guaranteed that they will end in disaster.

What happens in most partnerships is that one person puts in more and one person puts in less. Pretty soon, one of the partners feels victimized, which is often true. It's rare to find two people who are willing to work equally hard to make a business successful. One partner will invariably want to take more time off, which will increase the level of resentment by the one who stays to work.

Two people often enter into business partnerships because they like each other and think it would be a neat idea to start a business together. These partnerships, when they end, usually ruin the relationship between the partners, sometimes forever.

The only time that a business partnership is justified is when the partners have complementary skills and abilities. One person may be good on the technical side, while another is good on the marketing and sales side. In 1939, for example, William Hewlett and David Packard formed a business partnership, which became the Hewlett-Packard Corporation. Each of these men had skills and abilities that the other lacked, but together they formed the ideal top management team, and they went on to build one of the most successful companies in history. This is a rare exception.

The basic rule holds true: don't take partners. After all, you're going into business so you can have freedom and autonomy, so that you can be the master of your own ship, totally in control of your financial future.

Personal Loans

The next kind of money that you can get is personal loans from your banker based on your credit history and your personal collateral. You can get a personal line of credit or even a home equity line of credit while you're fully employed at another job.

In credit approvals, two years is the magic number. When you've been working for a company and living in the same place for two years, you can get all kinds of credit from credit cards and department stores, up through and including all kinds of personal loans, simply backed by your own personal guarantee. Consequently, the time to put all of your personal loans in place is before you leave your current job. Once you've borrowed the money, they're not likely to demand it back unless you're late in making your payments. So you can borrow to the maximum on just the strength of your name and your repayment history while you're still employed at your current company.

Here's another rule: guard your credit rating as a sacred thing. You have the right to demand a transcript of your complete credit rating from the credit bureau in the city where you live. Examine your credit rating at least once a year, and definitely before you start off to build your own business. Your credit rating becomes terribly important when you need to get any kind of financing as an entrepreneur. If there are any black marks on your credit rating, do everything you possibly can to remove them.

Borrowing from Banks

Here are some tips on borrowing from your bank as a businessperson, especially one building a small business. First of all, remember that entrepreneurs may be risk takers, but bankers are not; they are inherently conservative. They are successful to the degree to which they avoid risk in lending. The purpose of a commercial bank, and the job of the lending officer, is to make good loans. The banker that you talk to is judged by his superiors solely on the basis of the number of quality loans that he makes. If the banker makes a loan that goes bad—and many loans to small businesses do go bad—he will get a black mark on his record that will affect his pay scale, his position in the bank, and his likelihood of being promoted.

As a result, the easiest thing for a lending officer to do is to say no, because if he does, there's no way he can make a bad loan; he avoids risk by not making the loan in the first place. You must be aware of this when you go in. However, the good news is that bankers are in the business of making loans, and if you can convince them that there is no risk in lending to you, they may give you some of the money you need.

Select your bank carefully.

Once you decide to go into business on your own, select your bank carefully. Interview several bank managers or senior lending officers in advance of opening an account. When you visit the banks, tell them that you're going to be starting a new business and that you're looking for a bank where you can open your accounts and keep your money. Ask them about their policies towards small businesses, their lending practices, and especially their lending authority. Every loan officer, bank executive, and every bank branch has a lending limit: the amount that they are allowed to approve as a loan without recourse to higher authority. Some junior lending officers have a lending limit as low as $10,000. It's a good idea to ask each of the bankers what their lending limit is. They'll usually tell you honestly if you ask them.

The most important thing in dealing with a banker is the chemistry between you and the banker. The quality of the interaction, the relationship between the two of you, is perhaps the most important single factor in your decision about which bank to use and which banker to deal with. You must feel very comfortable and friendly toward the banker, and the banker must feel the same way toward you, or you may be getting into more trouble than you're looking for. Many businesses have been shut down by bankers who suddenly decided that they didn't particularly like the business owner. Several lawsuits have been triggered by these seemingly arbitrary behaviors. Your job is to make sure that you get along well with the banker before you take out a loan and maintain the relationship afterwards.

When you have finished interviewing different banks, you make your selection and proceed to open your personal checking, savings, and company account. Then invite the banker you've selected out to lunch. During the lunch, tell them about your business plans. Have your completed business plan and your personal financial statements, showing your assets, your liabilities, net worth, and your next year's budget projections to leave with him. Go over this material briefly and then let them look at it for a few days. Bankers have a process for evaluating a business plan. They have access to a good deal of confidential information on different types of businesses. After you leave, they'll compare your financial projections with what they think would be reasonable to expect in that business or industry.

One of the best rules in dealing with the bank is to ask for money when you don't need it. Once you've borrowed the money, repay it promptly. I once knew a successful entrepreneur who began borrowing and repaying money over a period of three years before he started his own business. He would purchase a certificate of deposit for $1,000 in a bank. Then he would go to the lending officer and pledge the certificate of deposit as collateral for a $1,000 loan. This is a very easy loan to get approved. He would then take the $1,000 out of the bank, take it across the street, and leave it in another bank for thirty days. Then he would come back and repay the entire amount plus interest. He would come back a month later to borrow $2,000, and later a $5,000 loan. Over the course of two and a half years, he was able to work up to a $25,000 unsecured loan based on his perfect record of repayment.

This is something you might do to build up a strong credit history before you go out on your own. When you open your account, request a personal line of credit. Whenever possible, meet and deal with the bank manager rather than with a lending officer. If you must deal with a lending officer, ask to be referred to a senior lending officer.

The Five C's of Loan Approval

Banks look for five essential factors when approving a loan. They are called the five C's of loan approval or disapproval.

First, they look at your *character*: your background and your reputation. They want to know who you are, where you've worked, and what you've done. Where did you go to school, and where do you live? What is your general reputation in the community?

Second, they look for your *capacity*, or your ability to repay the loan. Banks place a high value on your proven ability to earn a respectable amount of money. If you've worked and earned a good living for several years, this demonstrates to the bank that you have the capacity to generate sufficient cash flow to repay a personal or business loan.

The third factor that banks look at is your *collateral*: the assets that you can put up to secure the loan. It's not uncommon for a bank to initially require as much as five times the amount of the loan in the form of collateral. The very least that any bank will lend against is two to one. This means that you must have $2 worth of collateral that the bank can attach or put a lien on for every dollar that they'll be willing to lend you. If you have no track record at all in business, especially with a particular bank, they might require $3, $4, or $5 of collateral for every dollar they will lend you. Remember, their

---

The Five C's of Loan Approval

1. Character
2. Capacity
3. Collateral

4. Capital
5. Credit

primary concern is making good loans. A good loan is one where they get back all their principal plus interest.

Banks also look for primary and secondary sources of repayment. A person who asks for a business loan attempts to prove that the main or primary source of repayment will be the cash flow from the business. Then (although they seldom say it) bankers want to see your secondary source of repayment. In other words, how will the bank get its money back if your business fails completely? Most loan applications from businesspeople are turned down because the bankers are not convinced that the cash flow from the business is sufficient to ensure that the bank will be repaid. Whenever possible, be ready to offer a secondary source of repayment, either from the sale of other assets or from income from other sources.

The fourth factor that the banks look for is your *capital*. They will want to know how much you are personally planning to invest in this business. They want to know that you have "hurting money" in the business. They want to see that you have put in a good deal, if not all, of your own assets, and that your own financial future is on the line. Bankers know that they're much more likely to be repaid if your entire financial life depends upon the success of the business.

The fifth factor that the banker looks for is your *credit*: how well you've repaid any and all loans that you've made in the past. For lending officers, this is often the most important single part of the equation. It's often hard to assess your character or have any guarantee with regard to your capacity. Bankers don't like to seize collateral in the event of a loan not being repaid, and even if you have invested a lot of capital in the business, there's no way they can get their hands on it if things go wrong. The one thing that they can take to their lending committee is your credit rating, and they will do a detailed search of your credit history. That's why it's so important to keep it as clean as a whistle.

Supplier Financing

Another way to minimize your cash requirements when you start your business is to use *supplier financing*. Basically, this method consists of buying your products or raw materials from suppliers and then quickly selling the products to your customers before you have to pay your supplier for them in the first place. Many small companies have gotten started by arranging credit terms with the people who supply them with the essentials for their businesses. To do this yourself, you need a clean credit rating and a great personality. You need to visit your suppliers and sell them on the idea of extending credit to you. Sometimes they'll insist that you develop a three or six-month payment history with them before they can extend more credit.

Whatever it takes, resolve to build up an excellent supplier relationship. Develop personal friendships with the people who can make decisions on your line of credit. If you can buy and sell before you have to pay for what you bought, everything you make is straight profit. This is often called *kiting*: using someone else's money between when you've taken possession of the product and when you actually have to pay for it.

Guard your integrity as a sacred thing.

Your ability to kite with your suppliers will totally depend upon your character and your credibility. That's why it's so important to guard your integrity as a sacred thing. Suppliers talk to each other, and you will soon get a reputation that can either help or hurt you. Be sure it is one that helps you.

Another way to build your business with little cash is to ask your customer to pay for all or part of the order when he or she places it. Whenever you make a sale, ask for a 25 percent or 50 percent down payment or retainer. If the customer tells you they pay on a thirty-, sixty-, or ninety-day basis, throw yourself on their mercy: explain that you're a little guy, you're just starting off, and you would really appreciate it if they would pay you in advance.

Venture Capital

Many people who start businesses think they're going to raise the money they need from venture capitalists. The fact is that venture capitalists are some of the sharpest businesspeople in America. They look at about 100 business plans before they select one that they are willing to look at more closely. This means that 99 percent of all applications for venture capital are turned down for one reason or another.

Venture capitalists usually look for three things before they'll consider lending to a company. The first is a proven success record of a minimum of two years. They want to study the track record of your organization to be sure that you know what you're doing and can deliver on your promises. Venture capitalists are reluctant to fund a brand-new business, although they'll do so on occasion if the second and third factors are in place.

The second factor that venture capitalists look for is a complete business plan. They judge the business acumen and the quality of the entrepreneur based on whether the business plan is honest, factual, accurate, and complete. Many business schools train students on how to prepare business plans as a basic part of their education. As I've said before, don't underestimate the importance of preparing a detailed business plan.

The third factor that venture capital suppliers look for is a competent management team already in place. In fact, the management team has proven to be the critical factor in the success of many high-tech businesses.

The major downfall in going to venture capitalists for funds is that they will demand a large piece of your company, and they will almost always require that you give them control should things go wrong. Many entrepreneurs have been forced out of their own companies by their venture capital suppliers when they fail to meet their projections.

Entrepreneurs are frequently too optimistic with regard to sales and profits. It's much better to underestimate and come in early than to be too enthusiastic and fail to meet your target. Both bankers and venture capitalists will judge the quality of your management by how well you meet the numbers that you've projected. Bankers especially become very nervous when entrepreneurs don't achieve their goals in sales, cash flow, and profitability. Venture capitalists will often step in quickly to take over the company if you miss one or two of your financial targets. In order to avoid getting yourself into this unpleasant situation, it's far better to be conservative about your projections in the first place.

Whenever you borrow money from an institution, they will require you to submit complete financial statements every month. They will then sit down and compare your monthly financial results with your monthly financial projections. If your results are below your projections, they will start reaching for the plug. When bankers get uneasy about your ability to hit your numbers, they tend to panic so as to ensure that there is something to grab before the loan is irretrievably lost. If you doubt this, just ask any banker how he or she feels about a loan to a businessperson who is not meeting their numbers.

Treat your business like a turnaround.

Turning Around Your Business

One of the best attitudes towards starting and building your business is to treat it like a turnaround. A turnaround is a business that has gotten into financial trouble through mismanagement. When a company gets into a tough financial situation, the top management is often replaced by a turnaround specialist: an individual who can come in and act quickly to save the business. If you treat your company like a potential turnaround all the time, you'll always be assuring maximum profitability and minimum cost. Here are some of the things that a turnaround specialist will do when a business is running out of cash and is unable to make its payments or payroll:

1. The specialist will objectively assess whether or not the conditions or declining sales are long-term or short-term. The specialist will always assume the worst and proceed as though the worst were going to happen. If sales are declining dramatically, the specialist will assume that this is part of a larger trend and will act accordingly.

2. The specialist will immediately act to preserve cash at all costs, halting payments to suppliers and accelerating payments from customers wherever possible. Throughout your entrepreneurial career, you must treat cash as king. Hold on to it carefully, and

part with it reluctantly. A business with cash can survive almost any storm, but a business that runs out of cash can go under in a few days.

3. The turnaround specialist will even give discounts to customers for early payment. You should do the same thing. Get the longest possible terms in paying your suppliers and give the shortest possible terms in collecting from your customers. Give them 2 percent off if they pay within fifteen days. Many companies are set up to automatically pay early in order to take all discounts.

4. If you run into financial trouble, visit your banker immediately and tell them about the situation. Never let your banker first find out that you're in trouble by finding out that you've missed a payment. Be sure that your banker is the first to know. I've spoken with several bankers on this subject, and they all say that their first instinct will be to do everything possible to help the businessperson who lets them know in advance. But when they find out after the fact, they tend to become both scared and angry, and you can lose a lot of your ability to negotiate with them.

If you run into financial trouble, visit your banker immediately and tell them about the situation.

One thing that has saved me with my bankers when the cash dried up was to renegotiate my loans temporarily and pay interest only, suspending all principal payments for a certain period of time. As long as the borrower is making interest payments, the loan is considered a good one on the books of the bank. Bankers will almost invariably allow you to go to interest only payments if that's what you need to do to weather a period of cash shortage.

5. If negative conditions continue, turnaround specialists will lay off all nonessential staff and eliminate all nonessential expenses. They will cut everything to the bone rapidly. What you should learn from this is the motto *frugality*. In building your company, you should never have any nonessential staff or nonessential expenses. Insist on spending only what you absolutely have to in order to enable the business to function and generate sales revenues.

6. The next step a turnaround specialist would take is to sell off assets as rapidly as possible. If you ever get into financial trouble, assess the assets you'd be willing to sell in order to save your business; then begin to sell them immediately. Don't wait until it's too late and you have to let things go at bargain basement prices. The two major reasons businesses fail are lack of sales and poor cost control. A loss of sales momentum will cut off the incoming cash flow, causing the business to strangle. Poor cost control will cause too much money to be going out the back door, and even though sales are strong, the company can still go broke.

The two major reasons businesses fail are lack of sales and poor cost control.

The primary reason for poor cost control is that too much inventory is being ordered and too little of it is being sold. Once you've taken possession of inventory for resale, it's usually hard to give it back. It's essential to run your business lean and mean, spending only what you have to in order to move forward, and carrying only the inventory that you need to supply your customers in a timely fashion.

Finally, the turnaround specialist would get in, roll up his sleeves, and take control of all income and expenditures. He would insist upon approving every expense and signing every check. Nothing that did not absolutely have to be spent would be authorized. The turnaround specialist would be very hard-minded, even ruthless, with regard to cash outflows.

One of the smartest attitudes that you can develop is the attitude of the turnaround specialist. Continually look at your business from the outside and think of ways that you could make it more efficient. Think of ways to increase the cash flow and cut down on the cash outflow. Practice frugality in everything you do, and don't lose money.

The purpose of this chapter has been to open your mind to the fact that you don't need a lot of money to get started in a business of your own. More than anything else, you need guts. If you want to be financially independent, you'll never achieve it working for someone else unless you become a senior executive of a large corporation. The most certain route to riches in America is to start and build your own successful business. Don't let lack of money hold you back. Many of the most successful businesses in America have been built by men and women who started with nothing or were even deeply in debt. They didn't let that get in their way. They were so determined to take their idea to the marketplace that they couldn't be stopped by a little thing like shortage of cash. They started their business in their basements or on their kitchen tables. They worked out of their homes and cars. They worked in borrowed and rented spaces and in cold offices and warehouses. They negotiated with their bankers, suppliers, and customers to keep the cash coming in until they got the business off the ground.

They persisted and persevered until they started to make the profits they knew were possible. And they finally made it to business success and financial independence.

What someone else has done you can do as well. If you are serious about getting rich in America and the idea of entrepreneurship appeals to you, now is the time to take steps to launch yourself in your own business. It will be the greatest adventure of your life.

An Exercise

Now here's an exercise for you. Go through this chapter again, and write out all the ideas that you can think of to generate the cash you need to start your business. Look over all of your personal assets and assess your friends and relatives for how much you think you might be able to borrow from them. Call these people and tell them you might need to borrow some money in the future; would they be able to lend you a certain amount of money if you asked for it? This will give you a good idea of the resources that you can draw upon.

Another good exercise is to get your credit rating into excellent shape and begin building up your credit history at the bank you choose to deal with. Take out short-term cash loans based on your character and collateral; then pay them back. Arrange for personal letters of credit. If you have a home, take out a home equity line of credit if possible. Make all of the necessary financial arrangements before you leave the security of your current job. Every minute you spend preparing and strategizing for the launching of your new business is going to save you ten minutes or ten hours in making your business successful.

Major Points

- Your ambition and determination will determine your success.
- The best way to build your business is bootstrapping: investing your time rather than your money.
- Guard your credit rating jealously.
- Don't underestimate the importance of a detailed business plan.
- It's much better to underestimate sales and profits than to fail to meet your target.
- Hold on to cash carefully, and part with it reluctantly.
- Build and maintain a good relationship with your banker.

5

Get Your Message Across

Nothing happens until a sale takes place. The ability to sell is the critical skill for success in entrepreneurship. If you can sell well, you have the basic skills necessary to succeed at starting and building your own business. Fortunately, there's so much information available today on marketing and selling that you can learn how to sell well no matter where you're starting from.

In selling your product or service, the law of accumulation holds true: everything counts. Every time your company, products, services, people, or promotional materials come into contact with prospective customers, they leave an impression, positive or negative. They are either helping you to make sales or taking away from your sales.

A well-planned advertising and promotional sales strategy must be aimed at building the image and credibility of your company with every exposure. Your credibility, along with that of your company and your products and services, is the foundation of your success in the marketplace. People must believe in you and your company. They must trust you enough to select your product over those of your competitors.

Almost everything you do is selling you in some way.

Your Company Name

Almost everything you do is selling you in some way. Start with your company name. Choose it carefully in order to convey a message. Small companies should clearly state the type of business in the name. For example, if you're an accountant, you should call your business John Jones Accounting Services rather than John Jones Business Services or John Jones Enterprises. Be as specific as you can in the title. Only larger companies with established markets can use general names that don't refer to their specific product or service. IBM used to be called International Business Machines, a title that clearly told its customers what it sold and where it sold it. Only as the company became better known was it able to reduce its name to initials without losing its impact in the marketplace.

Your stationery, business cards, and logo should state clearly what business you're in. If possible, they should mention the products or services that you are offering. Everything that you produce should be selling all the time. It should have a message that enables a buyer to know what you are selling, and if possible, to give the customer enough information to take the next step toward a purchase.

Location, Location, Location

The location of your company's premises is terribly important if you're going to open up a retail business. In retail, the key to success is the same as in all of real estate: location, location, location.

The most important element of location in a retail business store is the traffic count: the amount of traffic that goes by the front door. It's possible to make serious mistakes in this regard. There are strip shopping centers that are located on the drive-home side of the road: people don't stop at these centers because they're on the way home, when people are not in the mood for shopping. Some strip shopping centers on the drive-to-work side of the road suffer from the same problem. They have lots of traffic going past, but the drivers are not in a mood to stop and shop.

If you're not in the retail business, the location of your premises is not particularly important. It's not necessary to locate in expensive office towers to make a positive impression on your prospective customer. Nobody's going to buy or not buy from you because you're paying a certain amount per square foot in rent. The purpose of a business is to create a customer, and every dollar that you spend should be aimed at creating customers in some way. If what you're doing doesn't have an immediate impact on sales, it's not a good promotional expense.

Three Basic Questions

Here are three questions that I put to anyone who has an idea for a new product or service.

The first question is obvious: Is there a market? Will people buy the product or service? In almost every case, the person with the idea will assure you that yes, there is a market. They have spoken to people who can and will purchase the product.

My second question is, is the market large enough? Are there enough people who will buy the product or service to make it a viable business idea? In many cases, businesses fall flat on this point.

Three Basic Sales Questions

1. Is there a market?
2. Is the market large enough?
3. Is the market concentrated enough?

There are a number of people who will buy the product, but the number is not large enough to justify starting a business to sell it.

My third question is often the killer: is the market concentrated enough so that you can reach it in a cost-effective way with advertising and sales? For example, there may be 100,000 people in the United States who can buy or use a particular product or service. However, they may be spread out, so there's only one such person per community across the entire country. Even though the market exists, it may be virtually impossible to sell to that market in a cost-effective way.

Advertising is selling without a salesperson.

Advertising

Which brings us to the question of advertising.

Advertising is how you tell your customers that your product or service is available, what it will do for them, and why they should buy it. Advertising is selling without a salesperson. Every advertisement should trigger the single response from a qualified customer: "That's for me!" If any advertisement doesn't trigger that reaction, it's a poor advertisement.

The basic rule is that creative advertising sells, period. If it doesn't cause a person to want to act immediately to purchase your product, then it's a bad advertisement, and you shouldn't spend any money on it. Many people who make their livings producing advertising for small companies are grossly incompetent. They produce what they consider to be clever or interesting advertising, but it doesn't sell.

The best way to test your advertising is to show it to people you know, including your spouse and friends. If they do not immediately respond by saying it's a great advertisement, don't spend any money putting it in front of customers who don't even know you.

Advertising, which is selling on paper or by radio, television, or online, is an investment. Like any other investment, it should have an expected return. When you spend a dollar on advertising, you should expect to earn a profit on the sales that you get from that advertising. If you don't, you should stop advertising in that medium or with that particular ad. For example, if you invest $1,000 in advertising and you earn a 25 percent profit on the sale of your products, you would have to sell $4,000 worth of your product—a $1,000 profit—to break even on the advertising. However, since advertising is a risk, you should expect to make $3, $4, or $5 in profit back from every dollar that you spend on it. In other words, if you spend $1,000 in advertising and you have a 25 percent profit on sales, you should expect to get $10,000 or $15,000 or $20,000 in additional sales as a result. If you don't, you're wasting your money.

Before you advertise, determine how much you can afford to lose. Every advertisement is a gamble. Sometimes you win. Sometimes you lose. Sometimes your advertising will give you a great response, sometimes none at all. You must be prepared for no response at all when you run any ad in any medium.

Estimate and determine your high, your medium, and your lowest rate of expected return on an advertisement. When someone is trying to sell you an ad, show them your expected rate of return and ask if it is realistic. Often people who sell advertising will become embarrassed when you ask this; they will be unable to continue the conversation because they know that very few companies get the kind of returns on investment in advertising that they need to justify the expense.

Never advertise on credit.

A good rule when you advertise is to always pay cash. Never advertise on credit. Many entrepreneurs make the fatal mistake of thinking they will pay for the advertisement with a profit they make from the sales that come as the result of the advertisement. This very seldom occurs. However, when you pay cash for your advertising, you tend to think more carefully about the amount you're spending and how you're spending it than if you buy it on credit.

Advertising Venues

Traditional advertising venues include, first of all, the newspaper. You only advertise there if you're trying to cast a wide net and if your product or service appeals to a large number of people whom you could reach effectively in no other way. Newspaper advertising can be very expensive as well as very effective. It can also be very expensive and not effective at all.

The second traditional medium is radio. The key to advertising on the radio is to select the station and program based on the demographic profiles of the listeners. For example, if you're offering a sporting product or sell sporting goods, you'd advertise on a radio station that has a lot of sports coverage. The key here is to request accurate information from the radio station on their Nielsen ratings, which will tell you exactly how many people listen to that station, as well as their ages, occupations, education, and income levels.

A third form of advertising is direct mail. The key advantage of direct mail is that you can make it very narrow and focused. You can buy carefully selected lists of specific customers who can and will buy your product or service. The key to using direct mail is to purchase a small number of names from a particular list and send out a test mailing to see what response you get before doing a larger mailing through a larger list. Remember, the secret to successful advertising is test, test, test.

To these venues must be added the Internet, which at this point is perhaps the single most effective way of advertising. But it involves many variables, such as search engine optimization, which are an enormous topic in their own right. Fortunately, you can research Internet advertising (not surprisingly) in many places on the Internet.

The small businessperson must do focused advertising that gets results immediately. You can use other forms of advertising as well, but they should only be used in conjunction with advertising in larger venues. You can send out flyers to homes in the neighborhood or community where your business is located: a shotgun approach that usually has a low rate of return. You can advertise in special interest magazines and trade publications for particular professionals who may need your product or service. You can use transit advertising—advertising that appears on buses or taxis—as well as outdoor signs. But these media are seldom effective all by themselves. You usually have to do a little of each in combination to make a significant impact.

Effective Advertising

To make an advertisement effective, here are the questions that you need to answer while preparing it. First, determine exactly what is to be sold. Second, determine to whom it is to be sold. Who's your customer? Whom exactly are you aiming this advertisement at? Third, determine exactly what action you want your customer to take as the result of seeing this advertisement, and then ask your customer to take that action in the ad. Say something like, "Pick up the phone and call us now" or "Come in before Saturday at 5 p.m. to take advantage of this special offer." Don't assume that your customers will figure out the required action for themselves. Be very specific in telling them what you want them to do.

**You always have to be answering the question,
"What's in it for me?"**

Fourth, determine what benefits you will offer to motivate your customer to take action. You always have to be answering the question, "What's in it for me?" Remember, your customer is reading dozens of other ads. The benefits that you offer for taking action must be more attractive than those offered by any of your competitors.

Fifth, in writing an ad, keep one theme dominant: your unique selling proposition. Each advertisement should make one specific proposition to the buyer. It should convey one specific message so that when the buyer turns away from the advertisement, that message sticks in his or her mind.

Finally, use straightforward, honest language that captures attention, creates interest, arouses desire, and asks for the sale.

Getting Free Publicity

Here are some ideas for getting free publicity to help you sell more of your product or service. The basic rule is that if you want publicity, ask for it. Newspapers especially need an enormous amount of material to fill their pages day after day. You should also try to get onto radio and television. If you have something of human interest, especially something unusual, you can launch a program to get free publicity, and you'll be amazed at how much you get. I have personally obtained many tens of thousands of dollars of free publicity by doing the things that I'm about to recommend to you.

Start off with a press release sent to every relevant medium in your market area, including newspapers, radio stations, and television stations, including community cable channels. Send it also to magazines and any other publications where it may be useful for you to get exposure.

The press release should tell about your new business or something new it is doing. You can send out a press release when you move to new offices, introduce a new product or service, upgrade an old product, hire a new person, or even when you embark upon a new promotional campaign. Any one of these can be construed as news if you describe it properly.

Write a 100-word description of your product or service, double-spaced. Include a good photograph of your product in use or of you delivering your product or service to your customers. Make your description short and factual. Don't try to entertain; instead give interesting information on how it works. Use a good three- or four-word headline on your press release, like, "New business breaks national record," or "First time in San Diego." At the top of the page, write, "For immediate release." Make it an informative news release rather than an ad. Don't try to sell your product; just try to make it interesting and different, and if possible, put some kind of a twist on it.

When you've written your press release, read it and ask, "Is this news?" News is timely: something that has just happened or has some association or relevance to current events. If you can make your product or service interesting and newsworthy, you can get lots of free publicity and trigger sales in quantities that will astonish you.

If you can get on to a radio talk show, make it easy for the interviewer to have you on. Send a list of questions for the interviewer to ask you. Be prepared to answer the questions with quick, punchy answers that are interesting for the radio listeners.

When you get on to a television show, do exactly the same thing. Create a ten- or twelve-question fact sheet to act as a prompter for the host of the show. Hosts of television interview shows are usually very quick on their feet. They can often glance at your list of questions, put it aside, and then shoot the questions at you for the next thirty minutes without missing a beat. When you get on to a television show, don't try to be an entertainer; sell by giving good, useful information to viewers. Remember, the person watching has a remote control in his or her hand. He or she is asking continually, "Why should I continue watching this show?" If you give useful and valuable information about how your product or service can benefit the listener, people will continue to stay tuned.

The sale is the culmination of all your efforts.

Twenty-Two Methods of Selling

1. Direct selling
2. Retail sales
3. Newspapers
4. Direct mail
5. Mail order
6. Party plans
7. Door-to-door sales
8. Co-op mailings
9. Government sales
10. Sales representatives
11. Chain stores
12. Discount stores
13. Supermarkets
14. Department stores
15. Wholesalers
16. Premiums
17. Advertising specialties
18. Franchising
19. Trade Shows
20. Shows, Fairs, and Exhibitions
21. Charities and Fundraisers
22. Online

The Adventure of Selling

Your adventure into entrepreneurship begins with a concept for a product or service that you can sell at a profit in a competitive market. Everything that you do between coming up with the idea and meeting the customer is preparing for the sale. The sale is the culmination of all your efforts. Your market analysis, financial projections, advertising, promotion, physical location, and your production of products and services are all in preparation for actually making a sale.

The primary reason for business success in America is the ability to get the goods out of the woods: to sell the product or service at the point of contact with the final customer and get paid for it. There are about twenty-two different ways to sell. You can focus on one of them, or you can use several. Most companies, however, only use one or two.

Direct Selling

The first and most popular form of selling in America is direct selling. This is person-to-person selling: a salesperson goes out and meets with a customer, makes a presentation, closes the sale, gets the order, and leaves with a check. This will always be the most popular kind of selling. Many of the great entrepreneurial success stories are based on the ability of a single person to convince people that they should buy and use a particular product or service. To be successful, you're going to have to become very good at this kind of personal direct selling—one-on-one.

Most salespeople are not properly trained in the methods of professional selling. Fully 95 percent of them could sell much more of their products or services if they were better trained and did what they were then taught to do.

One simple formula describes the four basic parts of the sales process, known as AIDA.

A stands for *attention*. Every sales effort must first succeed in getting the prospect to stop and pay attention to your message. The sales effort is useless unless you have grabbed the prospect's attention. We often call this *preoccupation breaking*: the first words you say should break the preoccupation of the customer. The best way to do this is to ask a question or make a statement that refers to a benefit or advantage that the prospect would like to enjoy.

AIDA: The Four Parts of the Sales Process

1. Attention
2. Interest
3. Desire
4. Action

The second letter, I, stands for *interest*. You arouse interest by showing the prospect how your product or service works or what it does. You show how it is new or cheaper or different from other products or services. The interest phase is where you talk about the features of the product.

The third letter, D, stands for *desire*. You arouse the desire to buy a product or service by explaining the benefits that the customer will enjoy from purchasing it. Features arouse interest, but benefits arouse the desire to purchase.

Two of the most powerful emotions that cause people to act are the fear of loss and the desire for gain. Many effective sales presentations focus on showing customers how much they will gain by going ahead or lose by not buying. Perhaps the biggest mistake that salespeople make is talking too much about what the product or service is and too little about how the customer will benefit from it.

A benefit-oriented presentation can be structured around other powerful buying motives as well. The need for self-preservation or safety is a powerful motivator, especially when children or family members are concerned. The need for security is another motivator, as is the need for prestige or success. People are motivated to do things that improve their health. The desire for riches and power provides a strong motive to act. The desire for companionship is a motivator; so are the desires for social status, popularity, self-esteem, or pleasure.

The fourth part of the sales presentation is the second A, which stands for *action*. Action means getting agreement from the customer that he or she wants the product or service. This is also called *closing the sale* or *getting the order*. In the final analysis, your ability to get a binding decision, to overcome hesitation and procrastination, is the real mark of how effective you are as a salesperson. That in turn will determine the success of your business.

Fortunately, the close of the sale is simply the natural conclusion of an organized sales presentation, but it takes place only when sufficient buying desire has been aroused.

One of the entrepreneur's most important responsibilities is to become excellent at selling. Entrepreneurs often make the mistake of having an idea for a product or service without any desire to go out and sell it. They approach me at my seminars and ask me where they can find good salespeople. I tell them that unless they are good at selling or have a partner who is excellent in sales, they have little chance in succeeding. Ideas are a dime a dozen. It's the ability to sell them that transforms an idea into a business.

Five Questions to Answer

Here are five questions that you must answer in the course of a sales presentation. Remember, customers are just like everyone else. They are lazy, greedy, ambitious, selfish, vain, ignorant, and impatient. They all want more security, comfort, leisure, love, respect, fulfillment, and power. They are also in a hurry, busy, and preoccupied.

Taking all of this into consideration, the first question that you must answer when you approach a prospect, either in person or

---

Five Questions to Answer in Sales

1. Why should I listen to you?
2. What is it?
3. Who says so?
4. Who else has done it?
5. What's in it for me?

through advertising, is, "Why should I listen to you?" Your opening remarks must answer this question. You must grab the prospect's attention and hold it until you've had an opportunity to explain why they should consider your offer.

Once you have the prospect's attention, the next question you must answer is, "What is it?" The answer to this question is your product or service and what it does and can do for the customer.

The third question you must answer is, "Who says so?" Customers don't generally believe or pay much attention to the claims of salespeople or advertising, but they do believe when someone else attests on behalf of your product or service. You need independent proof of some kind—or even a demonstration—to show your customer that what you say about your product is true.

The fourth question the prospect wants answered is, "Who else has done it?" Nobody wants to be a guinea pig. Nobody wants to be the first one to try a new product. To overcome skepticism, you need testimonials in the form of letters from satisfied clients, lists of customers who are already using your product, and even photographs showing customers using it. Good testimonials are extremely valuable in overcoming customer skepticism and building trust and credibility.

The final question that the customer wants answered is, "What do I get?" or "What's in it for me?" You answer this question by focusing on benefits: showing the customer how their most pressing need for enjoyment, satisfaction, gain, savings, security, or any other benefit can be met by using your product or service.

The secret to successful selling is to ask questions, probe carefully, listen attentively, and find out what the prospect wants or needs to accomplish. Your job is to find out the prospect's hot button. This is the key benefit or need that will cause them to buy your product or service. Often, this is simply your competitive advantage or your unique selling proposition, but you must find out what a particular customer wants or needs and demonstrate that your product or service will give it to them.

Retail Sales

The second way to sell your product is through retail sales in your own store or through other retailers. Many entrepreneurs get exclusive market rights for a product in a particular geographical area and then simply supply those products to retailers in the area. Often entrepreneurs and businesspeople will manufacture a new product for sale through retail stores. This is perhaps the second most popular route to entrepreneurial success in the sale of new or improved products.

Before you commit yourself to any product to be sold at retail, visit potential retail venues and ask them what they think about your product. Ask them how much they will pay and what else they have that would compete with your product. Remember, fully 80 percent of retail products developed by major corporations fail every year. You can't be too careful in doing your market research before you commit yourself irrevocably to a particular product.

Newspapers

The third way that you can sell is through the newspaper to generate direct responses, either in person or in the form of telephone enquiries that you can follow up directly. All newspaper advertising is aimed at getting the customer to act now, not tomorrow, not on the weekend, but immediately. If it doesn't achieve this goal, either change the ad or stop the advertising altogether.

Direct Mail

A fourth way that you can sell is through direct mail. As we have seen, direct mail allows you to pinpoint your market. Success in direct mail depends upon having a good list of qualified buyers and a product that is specific to that group of customers.

There are thousands of lists available in the United States, and there are even companies that do nothing but assemble and sell mailing lists; these are known as mailing list brokers. You can get lists of every kind of person who has ever engaged in every kind of activity imaginable. You can get lists broken down by zip code, by income grouping, by the amount that they spend each year in direct mail, and by 100 other categories. But as I said earlier, when you decide to use direct mail, be sure to test both the offering and the list before you start to mail in volume.

Mail Order

The fifth method of selling is through mail order. You can place small ads in selected or specialized publications that appeal to your customer group—and of course online. Mail order sales account for billions of dollars in sales each year.

Party Plans

A sixth way to sell products is through a party plan. Some product lines, such as Tupperware, beauty products, specialty food lines, and specialty clothing, can be sold in homes by having the hostess invite her friends in for a presentation. She then receives a premium or a commission on all sales. Many small businesses have become large businesses by recruiting people to sell through a party plan. If your product line lends itself to this kind of selling, you could experiment in your own community or your own neighborhood and see how well it works.

Door-to-Door Sales

A seventh way to sell a product is through door-to-door or office-to-office sales. This form of cold calling is a powerful method of direct selling if the product is right and the sales presentation is effective. Hundreds of millions of dollars' worth of encyclopedias, books, and other educational products have been sold door-to-door. This is not easy, but much of the fundraising activity in the United States, especially in organizations like the Girl Scouts, is based on door-to-door selling.

Co-op Mailings

The eighth way to sell your product or service is through co-op mailings. Many large mailing firms or other companies will enclose your product flyer with their mailing or invoices in exchange for a share of the gross sales. If you have a credit card, you'll often receive these co-op mailings with your monthly bill. The only cost to you is usually the cost of producing the mailing. The company who is sending out the billing gets their share of revenues from the successful sales of the product. The advantage to you is that you don't have to commit large sums of money until sales start to be made.

Government Sales

The ninth way to sell products and many services is through the government. Levels of government in America—federal, state, county, and municipal—are the biggest single customers in the entire nation. They spend hundreds of billions of dollars every year, and most of the money is spent with outside suppliers. If your product or service is relevant, you should approach various government offices and find out who makes the buying decisions. Many companies find opportunities to manufacture products and create services for government departments because of the volume in which they purchase. You can become financially independent if you can develop a product that can be used by a great number of government offices or departments.

Sales Representatives

The tenth way that you can sell is through sales representatives. Many professional salespeople work on commissions, selling several product lines and related areas. You can advertise for them online and in local newspapers. There's no cost to you for having this kind of professional sales force unless and until they make a sale.

The weakness with sales representatives is that because they represent several products, they seldom focus their energies on a single product unless it's very appealing to their market. You will also have to pay them a higher than average sales commission. Nonetheless, when you're starting out, this is a terrific way to get people selling your product all over the country.

Chain and Discount Stores

The eleventh way to sell your product is through chain stores. Many chain stores have hundreds of outlets. You only need to sell your product to one buyer in the head office and it will go into hundreds of stores automatically.

The twelfth way that you can sell is through discount stores. Discount stores prefer to carry products at below normal retail. Sometimes you can repackage or relabel your products for sale to discount stores so it won't hurt your sales at full retail by other methods. Sometimes you can change the name or the packaging or change the size, quality, or quantity of your product to sell them in large quantities to stores such as Walmart or Costco.

Supermarkets, Department Stores, and Wholesalers

The thirteenth possible sales method is through supermarkets. Supermarkets carry many nonfood items. If you can sell your product to a buyer for a chain of supermarkets, often they will put your product onto the shelves in hundreds of outlets.

You can also sell your product to department stores. Product buyers in department stores are very astute, and if they like your product, they can become major customers for you. Some of the most successful products in America achieve their high sales volume by being sold to and through department stores.

The fifteenth outlet for your product is through wholesalers. Many wholesalers will agree to carry your product to sell along with their other lines direct to retail buyers. To sell to wholesalers, your product pricing must be structured in such a way that both the wholesaler and the retailer can make the kinds of profits that are expected in your industry. Of course, you'll have to sell to wholesalers at below wholesale price. Everyone has to make a profit.

Premiums

The sixteenth way that you can sell your product, if it's appropriate, is as a premium. Many companies will purchase your product to give away as a prize, award, or bonus for purchasing something else. Sometimes a magazine company will give your product as a bonus for purchasing a subscription. A successful promotion I saw recently included a book of coupons for McDonald's if the customer opened up an account at a local bank. You can use your imagination to go out into the marketplace and find companies that could increase their business by giving away one of your products to new customers.

Advertising Specialties

The seventeenth way that you can sell your product or service is as an advertising specialty. Companies may purchase your product to imprint with their names and give away as gifts. These can take the form of ashtrays, pens, Frisbees, caps, and pocket calculators.

Every year you receive calendars in the mail from your suppliers. These are advertising specialties. The manufacturers went to various companies and got them to purchase the calendars as business gifts to help build customer loyalty. Today this advertising specialty field embraces thousands of products.

Franchising

The eighteenth sales method is franchising. Many businesses have the capacity to be franchised and rolled out to other areas. Franchise businesses account for more than 40 percent of retail sales in America today.

Trade Shows and Fairs

The nineteenth way to sell your product or service is at trade shows. Buyers from thousands of companies attend trade shows each year to find new products to offer through their wholesale and retail outlets. Use trade show directories to look up all the different shows that might carry products similar to yours and might be attended by people who could buy your product.

The twentieth means of selling your product or service is through shows, fairs, and expositions. You can exhibit your products at conventions and at fundraising shows. Almost every major convention in America has an exhibit area that it rents out. The people at these conventions—wholesalers, retailers, oil well drillers, insurance salespeople, corporate managers, and so on—visit these exhibits to look for new products and services that they can use in their businesses.

Charities and Fundraisers

The twenty-first sales venue is charities and fundraisers. You can often sell your product to charitable organizations who will then sell it as a fundraiser to their members. Many companies have generated tremendous sales by selling their products to a Chamber of Commerce or by manufacturing and producing candy, nuts, toys or other items that can be sold to raise funds for nonprofit organizations.

Online Sales

The last and perhaps most important sales venue is online. This method is growing in importance every year and has created fortunes for innumerable entrepreneurs. Again, the best place to research online sales possibilities is online.

To repeat what I said at the beginning, nothing happens until a sale takes place. Selling is the core function of the entrepreneur. You may only have an average product in an average market at an average or even above average price, but if you can sell, you can still build a successful business. There are endless combinations of ways that you can get your product to your customers, but in the final analysis, someone has to ask someone to make a buying decision. You have to be willing to ask the customer to give you the order; you have to be willing to close. You have to be willing to risk your ego in exchange for building your business. If you're willing to sell aggressively, continually, from morning to night, you have what it takes to become an entrepreneur.

An Exercise

Now here's an exercise for you. Take your business idea—the one that you arrived at as a result of the exercise at the end of the chapter 3— and work out an advertising and sales strategy for your product or service. How would you name your company? How will you sell your product? Which of the twenty-two different ideas discussed above seems to be most appropriate for you?

How will you advertise your product? What will be the cost of the various advertising media? What is there about your product that makes it interesting or different? What could you do to use this feature to get free publicity? Whom could you talk to in order to get more information?

With regard to your product or service idea, answer the five questions a customer would ask in a written essay form.

1. Why should I listen to you?
2. What is it?
3. Who says so?
4. Who else has done it?
5. What do I get? What's in it for me?

If you can answer all those questions satisfactorily on a sheet of paper and then give it to someone else and interest them in purchasing your product, you may be on your way to entrepreneurial success.

Major Points

- Your credibility is the foundation of your success.
- Like any other investment, advertising should have an expected return.
- The secret to successful advertising is test, test, test.
- If you want publicity, ask for it.
- The secret to successful selling is to ask questions, listen attentively, and find out what the prospect wants.
- The sales close only takes place when sufficient buying desire has been aroused.
- The key to closing the sale is to ask for it.

6

Your Financial Future in Real Estate

One of the high roads to wealth has always been the acquisition and development of good, solid, income producing real estate. In this chapter, I'm going to talk about the key things you must know to survive and succeed as a real estate investor.

I've had the experience of being a real estate agent, a broker, and an investor, and I have bought, sold, developed, and leased tens of millions of dollars' worth of real estate in the United States, Canada, and Mexico. I've made a lot of money for myself and others, and (I hate to admit) I've lost money making foolish decisions. I've also lost money making what appeared to be prudent decisions, but I got caught when economic conditions changed unexpectedly.

Here I want to give you some valuable advice for generating profits more often than losses should you decide to pursue your fortune in real estate. It's based on my own experience and that of many real estate investors, developers, speculators, and millionaires. It will work, if *you* will.

There's probably no area of investment where more myths prevail than in real estate. You'll hear people saying that 90 percent of all fortunes in America come from real estate, that they aren't making any more of it, that it is the surest route to financial independence for the average person, and that you can buy it with no money out of your own pocket, instead having your tenants pay it off for you.

These assertions are all partially true and partially false. Many fortunes in America are based on real estate, but in these cases it was usually purchased with cash flow from another business, whose profits were channeled into real estate.

It's also true that they aren't making any more real estate (at least not in the sense of any new land). But it's also true that in many areas, real estate values are declining and have been declining for years. The fact that it is sometimes scarce doesn't mean that it's necessarily desirable, much less going up in value.

It's also true that real estate ownership is one of the best ways to achieve financial independence for the average person. But in order to become a successful real estate investor, you're going to have to become very much above average in your knowledge and understanding of how the real estate market really works.

It's also true that you can buy real estate with little or no money down and have your tenants pay it off for you. But this is a long, hard process, which requires a tremendous amount of work and intelligent analysis on your part.

Real estate is one of the most dynamic and competitive fields in the country, and the industry includes some of the smartest, sharpest, most experienced business professionals anywhere. Yet every year, even in boom markets, these experts lose millions of dollars as a result of decisions and investments that turn out wrong.

Not long ago, I had a man in my office who had built an extremely successful toy company and sold it to a major multinational firm for $35 million in cash. Everyone told him that the best place to put his money was into real estate, so that's what he did. He kept on doing it for eight years until his money was all gone. Then he went back to work as a commissioned salesman, starting all over again.

If someone suggests that it's easy to be successful in real estate, don't believe it.

I have friends who have been real estate millionaires and real estate bankrupts, all in less than one year. One friend, an extremely experienced real estate professional, went from $7 million net worth to $3 million in the hole in less than eighteen months. So if someone suggests that it's easy to be successful in real estate, don't you believe it. There's no such thing as easy money. Nowhere in this entire book have I said it will be easy for you to achieve financial success. And this is equally if not doubly true in real estate.

Five Ways to Success in Real Estate

On the other hand, it certainly is possible to do well in real estate if you approach it as you would any other business. Here are the five basic requirements for success in real estate:

1. Write out clear, specific goals, and put timelines on them. Set goals for the amount of money you plan to save and invest in real estate and for the amount of real estate that you intend to purchase in the next three, five, and ten years. Then set a schedule for yourself, with deadlines. The very act of writing out a set of goals will make you much more likely to succeed.

Five Ways to Real Estate Success

1. Write out clear, specific goals.
2. Write out a detailed plan of action.
3. Learn every detail of the business.
4. Back your plans with hard work, sacrifice, and persistence.
5. Go in for the long term.

---

2. Write out a detailed plan of action, listing everything that you're going to do, organized by time and priority. The combination of goals plus detailed plans will give you a blueprint for real estate accumulation that you can begin to follow on a day-to-day basis.

3. Learn every detail of the business. Because the potential rewards are so high in real estate, they tend to go to those who have done their homework and paid their dues. It's very important to become an expert before you begin investing your time and savings in real estate acquisition.

4. Back your plans with hard work, sacrifice, and persistence. Going into real estate is very much like starting a business: there's a tremendous amount that you have to learn but can only learn by experience. There will be ups and downs, successes and reverses, and you must be willing to persist patiently throughout, knowing you will be successful in the end.

5. Get in for the long term, for a minimum of ten to twenty years—that is, if you are serious about building up something lasting and worthwhile. Real estate investment is not something to jump into and out of. You step into it carefully while being prepared to hold on to it for a long time.

A recent study concluded that many people buy real estate, hold it for a long time, and then sell it just before it starts to rise rapidly in value. They become impatient when they hear other people tell stories of how quick or easy money was made by flipping real estate properties. They then sell an excellent property and put the money into something that may not be as good. Often, one or two years later, the piece of real estate that they sold increases in value by three, five, or even ten times. This is especially true with regard to raw land.

Real Estate Is Its Future Earning Power

Let's begin with a definition of investment real estate in its simplest terms. *Real estate is its future earning power*—nothing more and nothing less. The value of any piece of real estate is determined by the income that it can generate when it's developed to its highest and best use from today onward into the indefinite future. The value of a home is the value that a person who desires to live in that home will pay for. The value of a rental property is determined by how much people will pay to rent that property. The value of a piece of agricultural land is determined by the quality, quantity, and value of the crops that can be raised on that land. Millions of acres of land throughout the United States will never have any value, such as desert or swampland, because they cannot be developed to produce income or satisfy human needs.

Always ask, when and how will income or wealth be generated on or by this piece of property? The correct answer to that question tells you how much the property is worth today and how much it's likely to be worth in the future. There are vast areas of many large cities where property values are declining because growth and development have come and gone and will probably not return in the foreseeable future. Every day, men and women are selling homes and properties for less than they paid or are losing them to foreclosure because they have declined in earning power and therefore in value. Thousands of homeowners walk away from their homes each year because the value of those homes has declined to the point where they are not even worth the first mortgages that have been placed on them.

Buying Fixer-Uppers

Now that I have issued this warning, there are many things that you can learn and do, starting with very little money, to begin building your financial independence in real estate. If you have little money but lots of time, the simplest way to start is by using the Nickerson method. This is the process of buying homes that need work and fixing them up, thereby increasing their value. Here are the six steps you must follow to use this strategy successfully.

1. Do your market research. Look at houses until you find one that is underpriced relative to the neighborhood because it's rundown and needs a lot of work. A house that is underpriced sells for 20 percent or more below what similar houses are selling for in the same area based on the price per square foot. Real estate agents call this type of house a "handyman special," or sometimes they advertise it as a "starter home needing TLC" (tender loving care).

2. Purchase the property for the lowest possible cash down payment, and get the seller to carry back a second mortgage or trust deed on the property. Your ideal in investment real estate

---

How to Make Money from Fixer-Uppers

1. Do your market research.
2. Buy the property for the lowest possible amount of cash down.
3. Move into the property and refurbish it in your spare time.
4. Sell or rent out the refurbished property at a profit.
5. Repeat this process.
6. Move up to larger, multiunit properties.

---

is always to get the best price and terms, which are often more important than any other single factor. If you can get a low enough price and generous terms, you can make almost any property into a successful investment.

3. Move into the house, and renovate and refurbish it in your free time, doing all or most of the work yourself. Many husbands and wives have launched themselves toward financial independence by working together as a team to buy and fix up houses, approaching it as a family project.

4. When you have fixed up the house and yard so they're attractive, you can do one of three things: (1) sell the house for more than you paid, take the profit from the sale, and buy another house to renovate; (2) rent out the renovated house at a rate that covers your mortgage payments and perhaps gives you extra cash flow; (3) rent out the house and refinance it, often for as much as you paid, based on the higher earning power of the property when rented out to a tenant.

Let's say that you bought a house for $100,000, you negotiated well, and you only had to pay $5,000 down. The bank would give you a first mortgage of 80 percent or $80,000, and the seller would take back a second deed of trust in the amount of $15,000. You now own a $100,000 house with only a $5,000 investment. You move into it for two or three months and spend another $5,000 fixing it up. You find a tenant who will pay you $1,200 a month in rent for this newly renovated home. You can then often go to the bank and apply for a new first mortgage in the amount of, let us say, $90,000 based on the rent you are receiving. Say that a $90,000 mortgage would cost approximately $900 per month to service. If the bank agrees to refinance and issue you a new first mortgage for $90,000, you would get back your $5,000 down payment and your $5,000 investment in repairs and renovation. You would in effect, have no money of your own invested in the house at all.

On top of that, if your tenant was paying you $1,200 per month, you would have a positive cash flow from that house of $300 per month, with no money of your own in the deal. You could use that positive cash flow to pay off the $15,000 second deed of trust.

As you can see, if you did this once every six months, over the next ten years, you could end up with a cash flow of several thousands of dollars per month and a portfolio of properties in which you had little or no investment. This is the miracle working power of this method.

5. You can repeat this process with another house. Again, invest your sweat equity or your human capital in the renovation until you're ready to sell, rent, or refinance the house.

6. As you increase your assets, cash flow, and experience, move up to buying and fixing duplexes, triplexes, fourplexes, and eventually apartment buildings.

The two main advantages of this method are: (1) you can do it while you keep your full-time job, continuing to generate cash flow from your job for repairs and renovation; (2) you can start small, with little or no money and little or no risk, and expand your activities as you gain more knowledge and experience.

The one limitation of this method is that it takes an enormous amount of time to seek out and purchase the types of houses that are ideal for this process. But if you have lots of time and little money, you can start here toward financial independence.

Buying with No Money Down

Now let's talk about buying real estate with no money down. Certainly it's possible to buy real estate, especially older homes, with no money down, but that doesn't mean that it's easy.

Buying a house with no money down simply means finding someone who is eager to sell their house and is therefore willing to carry back a second mortgage on the property rather than demanding cash. Such a person is called a *motivated seller*, and finding such a seller is usually the only way to buy real estate with little or no money of your own.

For example, a house might be for sale for $100,000. Let us say that you can qualify for an 80 percent mortgage on the property. If the person selling the property will carry back a $20,000 second mortgage, you can end up owning the house (subject to the mortgages and payments) with no money out of your own pocket. If you could turn around and rent out the house for an amount high enough to cover mortgage payments, taxes, and any future repairs, your tenants would eventually pay off the cost of the house, and you would own it with no money down.

This method requires achieving a monthly rental rate equal to approximately 1 percent or more of the purchase price of the house. For example, if the purchase price of the house was $100,000, you would have to get a rent of approximately $1,000, or 1 percent of $100,000 per month, in order to service the debt on both mortgages. This strategy only works with lower-priced houses, because you can rarely rent out a more expensive house for enough to cover all the payments. Lower-priced homes also sell the most rapidly and are the most easily rented in almost any market.

If you didn't want to rent the house right away, or if the house was not yet suitable for renting, you could move in, make the payments while fixing it up, and then either resell the house or rent it out for enough to earn a profit. Or you could refinance the house based on its new cash flow from a new tenant paying a higher rent.

In his books *Nothing Down* and *Creating Wealth*, Robert G. Allen, the famous real estate investment advisor, suggests that you aim to buy a minimum of one or, even better, two houses per year with minimum or zero down payments. He suggests that unless you have a lot of time, you buy a house that requires little or no work so that you can immediately turn around and rent it out when you take possession.

Allen describes what he considers to be the ideal target property or investment grade property: a three-bedroom, single-family detached house or condominium that is located in a stable neighborhood within a five-mile radius of your own home that is worth at least 10 percent more than your cost, that you can buy with less than 10 percent down, and with terms which allow you to rent the home out with no negative cash flow or balloon payments coming due in less than five years.

Allen goes on to suggest that you only buy homes in the bottom end of the price pyramid, which is where most of the demand is. Lower-priced properties are the easiest to rent and have the greatest potential for upward price movement.

One basic rule of real estate is that you should only buy property that you can drive out and look at. The worst mistakes are made by people who buy property a long way from where they live. There are just as many real estate opportunities within driving distance of your home as there may be in another community or on the other side of the country.

Five Ways to Purchase with No Money Down

In looking for a house to purchase with little or no money down, there are five factors that you need to take into consideration:

1. The seller's motivation and flexibility. Do they want to sell in a hurry? And is the seller flexible enough to consider carrying back a second mortgage on the property? One successful real estate investor I know won't consider making an offer on a property until it's been on the market for at least six months or until the owners have already moved away and are extremely anxious to sell.

Five Factors in Purchasing with No Money Down

1. The seller's motivation and flexibility
2. Location
3. Financing
4. Price
5. The condition of the property

---

2. The location, as I'll talk about later in greater detail.

3. The financing or the terms. If you can get a property with the right terms, you can pay a higher price. If a house is worth $90,000 and the seller is demanding the full price, this would not normally be a bargain. However, if the seller will carry back a note for the amount above the first mortgage for five years with interest only and a balloon payment after five years, this then becomes an attractive purchase opportunity.

4. The price. You're looking for a bargain, that is, a house that the seller will part with for 90 percent or less of the going market price.

5. The condition of the property. You must always confirm this for yourself in detail.

So if you have a motivated and flexible seller with a house in a reasonably good neighborhood who is willing to carry back a second mortgage and sell the house at a reasonable price and the house is in good condition, you have all the factors that you need to make an excellent real estate purchase.

If you're going to get into buying and renting houses as a full- or part-time occupation, the best strategy is to buy one or two houses a year for the next ten years. During this period of time, your tenants will be making all your payments.

Except in the rarest of circumstances, you should never purchase an income producing piece of property where the debt service is not covered by the rent. Avoid negative cash flow at all costs: it causes more real estate entrepreneurs to go bankrupt than any other single factor.

Where to Find Properties

Where do you find homes to buy for no money down? Online resources are today probably the most common and productive sources, but there are other sources as well. For example, read all the real estate advertisements in the newspapers and the smaller neighborhood papers. Look on the bulletin boards in supermarkets in areas that you've decided are good choices.

Then drive through your chosen neighborhood and take down the phone numbers of every house for sale, especially those listed as for sale by owner. Third, contact every Realtor in the area and tell them exactly what you're looking for: bargain properties with low down payments. Tell them that you're looking for people who need or want to sell in a hurry and that you're ready to make a decision quickly. Fourth, you can run your own ad, asking for income producing properties. You can even say something as simple as "I buy houses; phone me," and put your phone number in the ad.

You can also have business cards printed with the title "real estate investor" on them and give them to everyone you talk to. Visit every bank in and around the area where you intend to invest. If there are community bulletin boards, write up a notice offering to buy homes and post it on every board, giving your phone number.

Just for practice, you can respond to ads that say, "For sale by owner." Ask the person who answers how much they want for the property and whether they would be willing to sell with a minimum or zero down payment. Often, if a person is motivated to sell, they'll accept any offer that enables them to get their full price. They'll even give you the house with no money down if you can assure them that you'll be able to make the payments that you commit to.

Pitfalls and Dangers

The pitfalls and the dangers in buying real estate with no money down are as follows: First, if a house is priced reasonably in a normal market, the seller will not have to accept no money down. The seller can get cash to mortgage or refinance the house himself. Many people, when you talk to them about selling their houses with no money down, will laugh in your face and even hang up the phone. Don't worry; you're looking for a motivated seller, and you may have to kiss a lot of horny toads before you find the handsome prince.

The second danger in this strategy is that you must be able to generate sufficient income to make the payments on both the first and the second mortgages. If you can't make the latter, the seller will have the right to step in and foreclose and take the house back from you. Many people who go out and find sellers willing to accept no money down end up losing both their money and their reputation when they're unable to keep up the payments. This is why it's so important to build up a cash reserve and never part with all your cash.

The third pitfall of buying real estate with no money down is that if you rent the house out to a tenant, the tenant had better be able to pay the rent; otherwise, you'll have to come up with it or else lose the house. Also, your tenant must not do anything to damage

---

Four Essential Things to Know in Property Buying

1. The economy of the community and neighborhood
2. The factors that make a property valuable in a specific area
3. How to evaluate and appraise real estate
4. How to negotiate and sell

the property, or its value will go down, and you'll end up owing more than the house is worth. And renters do damage rental property. Sometimes they even destroy it. Selecting your tenants very carefully and doing a detailed check on their background references is essential. "No references, no rental" should be your rule.

Four Things You Need to Know

Here are four things that you'll have to learn in order to make money in real estate:

1. You'll have to study the economics of the city and the neighborhood where you're thinking of investing. Some cities, and some neighborhoods in some cities, are in decline. They are risky choices for real estate speculation. Other cities and certain parts of cities are stable or growing and are therefore good areas for investment.
2. You'll have to learn about the factors that make a property valuable in a specific area. Why is one house more desirable than another? With experience, you'll be able to drive down a street and pick out houses that are excellent investment opportunities.
3. You'll have to learn how to evaluate and appraise real estate in order to be able to determine what kind price you can afford to pay.
4. You'll have to learn how to negotiate and how to sell people on the idea of dealing with you—especially the idea of giving you an excellent price or excellent terms, or both.

Ten Factors in Urban Economics

Let's start off with urban economics. What makes one city a better bet for real estate investment than another? Here are ten factors to consider when choosing a city to invest in:

1. The general level of business activity nationally. Nationwide recessions and depressions hurt all real estate everywhere. Almost invariably, nationwide recessions are triggered by rising interest rates. No matter where you are in the country, when interest rates go up, real estate values are hurt. So you have to ask, what is the overall national economy like today? And what do I think it's going to be like in the next few years?

2. The level of local business activity. This is often more important than the economic condition of the nation as a whole, because there are always cities, states, and regions that are growing while others are stagnant or declining. Perhaps the most important specifics are the number of business startups and the growth rate of the local economy, especially the unemployment rate. An area that is strong has a business start-up rate equal to 3 or 4 percent of the total number of businesses in the region. It will also have unemployment rates lower than those of the national economy.

3. Changes or potential changes in community employment and income sources. Where are the jobs now, and where will the jobs come from in the future? Are business and industry moving in or out? Are government offices and departments expanding or contracting? The single factor that has the greatest impact on the economic health of a region and its real estate values is the number of jobs existing and being created in the area. Wherever there is strong job creation, you have a strong economy and strong real estate values.

4. Area trends in financing terms and interest rates. Are the terms getting better or worse? Are interest rates rising or falling? How much will you have to pay as a down payment? What kind of terms can you get? What interest rates will you have to pay both

on first and second mortgages? In parts of some cities, the prices, terms, and interest rates can be more favorable than in other parts of the same community.

5. The rate of population growth or decline. Real estate values increase at approximately double the rate of population growth. For example, if the population increases 3 percent in an area, real estate values for single-family homes will increase at approximately 6 percent. Another rule of thumb is that real estate values increase at approximately three times the rate of inflation. If inflation is 3 percent per annum, real estate value should increase at the rate of 9 percent per annum. Real estate booms occur when both population increase and inflation take place simultaneously. A 3 percent increase in population per annum and a 3 percent increase in inflation per annum will equal a total of a 16 percent increase in residential real estate prices per annum.

6. Changes in the tastes and preferences of home buyers. What kind of homes do people want now? What size? What layout? What kind of homes are they likely to want in the future? What are the trends in new home construction? You must think about any property that you're considering purchasing as though you are going to own it for the next twenty years. You are buying the future earning power of the property. Look at it in terms of how it will measure up five or ten years from now in terms of customer taste and preferences.

7. The volume of building activity, construction cost levels, and the trends of those construction cost levels. How many new homes are being built each year relative to the absorption rate of new homes? The absorption rate is the number of new houses that are purchased for people to live in each year. If you have an

absorption rate of 3,000 homes per year and you have 3,000 homes being built, you will have a stable if not rising real estate market. But if you have a situation such as once happened in Phoenix, where there was an absorption rate of 8,000 homes per year and a construction rate of 12,000 to 15,000 homes per year, you're going to have strong downward pressures on both home prices and rental rates. Eventually there will be a real estate recession.

8. The vacancy rate. This is perhaps the single most important factor that influences real estate trends. When vacancy rates get below 5 percent, developers begin building more homes and apartments to satisfy the demand. When vacancy rates rise above 10 percent, developers stop building, and landlords begin to lower their rents and increase incentives to attract tenants. High vacancy rates are a high negative factor, making buying and renting residential real estate less desirable.

9. The interrelation between prices, rents, and construction costs. These are important to market conditions. When rents rise above a certain point, construction activity will tend to increase. When prices of real estate rise or fall above or below a certain point, construction of new residential accommodation will also decline or increase. Familiarize yourself with these numbers and ratios so you can be in a position to predict what's going to happen.

A number of years ago, I invested in a hotel in a small community. I foolishly entrusted this investment decision to my partners, all of whom were real estate professionals. It seemed like a tremendous deal going in, but they had overlooked one important factor: the economy of the town was both seasonal and unpredictable. It depended on government spending to maintain high levels of employment, and economic activity was partially determined by the prices of natural resources as well. All at once, the government cut back its spending and natural resource prices fell through the floor. Economic activity in the community dropped dramatically, and the hotel began sitting empty month after month. Failing to evaluate these factors in advance cost me more than $100,000 in less than a year. I finally lost the hotel to foreclosure.

Another relationship that you should study is the difference between the listing prices of homes and their final sales prices. In a strong market, houses will sell for between 90 and 100 percent of the asking price. In a weakening market, houses will begin to sell at between 80 and 90 percent of their asking prices. Even a 1 percent change in the average selling price compared with the asking price, either up or down, can indicate the trend in the real estate market. If you can spot a trend before it gets going, you can make or save yourself a lot of money.

10. The volume of market activity as reflected in the number of deeds recorded, the number of mortgages recorded, and the volume of foreclosures recorded at city hall. All of this information is on public record and is available to you for the asking.

The key is to compare the present level of market activity with previous levels, not only with previous years, but also with previous months. You want to be well aware of how long it takes to sell houses in different price ranges. For example, if you're looking for houses in the $150,000 to $175,000 price range, pay close attention to how many weeks or months on average it takes a house like this to sell after it comes on the market. If the selling time stretches out to three or four months, you'll be able to find more motivated buyers than if the selling time is only two weeks.

Another rule for residential real estate investment: people pay for homes in direct proportion to how close those homes are to where they work. This also applies to apartments and office buildings. Since people spend one third of their time at home and one third of their time at work, they will pay a premium to be able to live where the two are as close together as possible.

Here's another rule: when jobs increase, wage levels increase, or interest rates go down in a particular community, any or all of these will cause housing prices and demand to go up. Your job is to be alert to the level of job growth, how much those jobs are paying, and the trend in interest rates. A small bit of information can often be worth many thousands of dollars to you in buying residential real estate correctly.

Seven Key Factors for Growth

Here are the seven key factors that give a city the power to grow and enjoy increases in real estate value.

1. The economic and political power to attract business and industry. There must be reasons for businesses to move there, start up, and invest and expand. Business growth leads to population growth, which leads to growth in real estate values. Economic power in a city can come from a major industry that requires a tremendous number of service industries around it, such as the Boeing Corporation in Seattle. Political power can be based on the ability to move federal or state government facilities to a particular area, as happens in states and cities that have powerful friends in Washington or state capitals.

2. Dynamic community leaders, aggressive politicians, and active entrepreneurs. You're looking for a city where the mayor and

the council are prodevelopment, probusiness, and pro–free enterprise. The powerful people in the community should be strongly in favor of its prosperity through economic growth and development.

3. The labor pool, especially an educated, professional labor force. This is considered the single most attractive factor in determining where new companies will locate their head offices or expand. There seems to be a direct relationship between the percentage of colleges and universities in a city and the number of educated people in the workforce. Therefore, any city that has its fair share of colleges and universities is usually going to be a strong place to invest in residential real estate.

4. The fourth factor that gives a city the power to grow is the ability to export more goods and services than are imported into the area. If you look upon a city as a small nation, this is called having a *positive balance of payments*. When a city has the ability to command income from beyond its borders or city limits, it to takes in more money than it sends out. That extra money, kept in the community, will be reflected in higher real estate prices.

5. The ability to attract or generate new sources of income and employment or new business formation. This is considered the number one variable in determining a community's overall economic activity. The average community loses approximately 8 to 10 percent of its jobs by natural attrition each year. Companies shut down, fold up, go broke, or move away. Because of this, the number of jobs lost, plus more besides, must be created each year in order for a city to continue to maintain a vibrant economy. The basic requirement is that there must be new business formation at the rate of 3 to 4 percent per annum. For example, if there are 100,000 businesses in a given area, 3,000 to 4,000

new businesses must be formed per year for the region to maintain employment for its workforce and continue growing. If the rate of new business formation falls below 3 percent per annum, the unemployment rate will go up, and residential housing prices will start to soften or decline.

6. One of the most important factors in a city is the quality of living conditions and lifestyle. People prefer to live in cities that have beautiful weather and excellent environmental conditions, such as nearby beaches and mountains. The quality of local government and community tax levels are also important. The Sunbelt areas of the Southeast and the Southwest are growing more rapidly than any other part of the country primarily because of lifestyle considerations. People like to live where it's warm and sunny much of the year. In fact, as long as lifestyle is a major consideration, investing in residential real estate in the Sunbelt is a smart thing to do if you pick the property intelligently.

Here's another rule for real estate and economic decision-making that has changed my life twice and made many people rich: you can make more money in five years in a dynamic, growing city or region than you could in twenty years in a dying city or even in one that's leveled off.

You can make more money in five years in a dynamic, growing city or region than you could in twenty years in a dying city.

Inspirational speaker Earl Nightingale once told the story of a young man who sought advice from a wealthy older man. He told the older man that he badly wanted to become wealthy and asked him what he should do. The old man told him that it was easy to become wealthy: all he had to do was find a rapidly growing community and move there. Then he needed to save at least 10 percent of everything he earned and carefully invest it in real estate around the edges of the growing city. If the young man were to do this, in twenty years he would be wealthy.

But the young man replied, "That would require that I move away from my family and friends and start over again. I can't do that."

"Then," said the older man, "you really don't desire wealth as much as you say you do."

The moral of the story is simple: nothing in the world can stop you from becoming wealthy if you are willing to make the necessary sacrifices. But most people are not willing to make any sacrifices at all, much less those necessary to achieve financial independence.

Key Factors Affecting Real Estate

Here are the key factors affecting residential real estate investments:

1. Each property is unique. It is unlike any other. It is immovable, occupying a specific spot on the earth's surface. That's why it said that the three key factors in real estate are location, location, location.

2. Many owners have a sentimental attachment to their properties, and their ideas of value are distorted by their emotions. Homes are very emotional possessions, and often people are blind to what the house is really worth. Often a person will set a price on their house that is determined by what they have heard someone else got when they sold theirs. The two houses may have little in common; nonetheless, the owner will insist on getting that price, no matter what.

3. Buyers for a particular house are limited to people living in or near the community, or to people who want to move into that area. No matter how attractive the house is, only a certain number of people will be interested in that particular neighborhood in the first place. An attractive home in a distant location will sell for far less than the same home in a growing city.

4. Prices are affected by the terms and availability of financing. People buy payments as much as they buy the house; that is, they buy as much as they can afford to make monthly payments on. Lower interest rates translate into lower payments and faster sales. More people can afford the payments on more houses when interest rates are declining than when they're rising.

5. Zoning laws. Many communities have stringent zoning laws that make it difficult to renovate or upgrade a property. Other communities have loose zoning laws, which allow people to do whatever they want to do to their properties, often to the detriment of the whole neighborhood.

6. The value of any property is influenced by the character and appearance of the entire neighborhood and the overall economic outlook for that neighborhood.

7. The seventh factor to consider is that buildings are all different. Some have hidden defects, and some have exceptionally favorable features. When you're thinking of buying a house, you should never judge by appearances alone. Even if it looks great, it may have many problems that you cannot see from the outside.

8. There may be periods of rapid turnover in a particular area and periods of stagnation and decline. If you're serious about getting rich in real estate, you should seek to invest in a stable community with a solid economic base. Avoid communities that

are known for boom-and-bust cycles. In an unstable economy, it's too easy to lose the results of all your hard work.

9. Property values may be affected by the quality of police and fire protection in the area. Low-crime areas are more desirable than high-crime areas. Areas that are known to have good fire and police protection are more attractive to homebuyers and renters than areas that have a lesser reputation.

10. Property values are affected by the availability of water, sewer, gas, electricity, and the cost of those services. In some communities, they are less expensive, and in some communities, they are astronomical. Find out what it costs to run the utilities in a home that you're considering buying. Ask for the house's utility receipts for an entire year so that you can check seasonal fluctuations.

11. Air, water and noise pollution may have highly adverse effects on a home. One of the most desirable features of a house is that it is quiet and is located in a quiet neighborhood. If it is close to a freeway or a main traffic artery, there can be a continual roar of traffic that never lets up and makes the house less desirable. I've seen many houses that had to be sold at a steep discount because of traffic noise from nearby roadways.

Does this all begin to sound complicated? Well, it *is* complicated, but it's necessary. My job is to equip you with the mental tools that you need to be successful in real estate. I would be letting you down if I didn't point out some of these key factors for your consideration.

Remember, the only thing easy about money is losing it. Making money in anything, especially real estate, is hard work and requires careful preparation plus eternal vigilance.

Everyone with a property for sale wants to get as much of your money for it as they possibly can. Your job is to see that they don't.

Real estate investing must take into consideration the factors I've just discussed, whether it's a matter of a single-family house, a high-rise apartment, a single-tenant store, or a high-rise office building.

A Powerful Rule

Here's the key rule for real estate investment. Write it down. Carve it onto the outside of your checkbook. Here it is: You make your profit when you buy real estate, not when you sell. You make your profit in real estate by buying right, by buying the right property at the right price and terms. When you sell, you simply realize the profit that you really made at the time of purchase.

Never forget this rule. Many inexperienced real estate investors make the mistake of operating on "the greater fool theory" when they buy a property: they convince themselves that no matter how bad or overpriced the property is, there will always be a greater fool who will come along to rent it from them or to take it off their hands at a higher price. This theory is one of the primary reasons so many people end up losing money in real estate or any other type of investment.

**Don't become emotional about a property
that you are purchasing for investment.**

Another important rule: don't become emotional about a property that you are purchasing for investment. Always look at it from the viewpoint of a critical purchaser. Ask yourself, who will buy this property from me, and why will they buy it? Who will rent this property from me, and what features will they find attractive? In every real estate investment, put yourself in the position of the person you will eventually sell the property to; look at it through their eyes.

Choices of Neighborhoods

Now let's look at some additional factors affecting the choice of a specific neighborhood to invest in. First of all, in every city, whether it is growing or declining, there are neighborhoods that are also growing or declining. The patterns of growth or decline in a city are largely determined by the city's growth pattern out from the central core. This growth pattern in turn is largely determined by the topography, or the presence of rivers, hills, valleys, oceans, and swamps.

The basic growth pattern of a city is the expanding pie pattern. Imagine your city as a pie cut up into slices. As the city expands, the type of development in each slice tends to expand outward with it from the core. If a slice starts as industrial, it will tend to continue to expand as industrial. If it starts as high-quality residential, the outer edges of that slice will tend to continue expanding as high-quality residential.

Gradually, a core dying area will develop around the central business district as people, businesses, and commercial development expand toward the suburbs. You can often pick up real estate bargains in these declining areas. But remember, you are purchasing the future earning power of the property and the neighborhood. In a way, you're buying a share of stock in that area, just as you would buy a share of stock in a company. Your first job is to determine that the neighborhood is holding or increasing its appeal and attractiveness as time passes.

The best way to evaluate a neighborhood is to walk through and get a feel for it. Look for evidence that people are renovating and upgrading their properties. Listen for noise and pollution levels. Talk to the corner grocer, the person at the gas station, and especially real estate agents. Take the name and phone number of every real estate agent who has a home for sale in the area that you're looking at, call them up, and quiz them. Ask them every question that you can think of about the neighborhood. Usually real estate agents are your best source of timely and accurate information for a particular area. Learn everything you can, just as though you were going to buy a house, move in, and live there for twenty years, because the profit that you can make on any home you buy will depend on someone moving in for the long term.

The Rule of 100

Once you have found a solid neighborhood in a solid city with a strong, diversified economy, it's time to begin looking for a house to buy and either fix up or rent. This leads to my rule of 100: expect to look at 100 houses before you are knowledgeable enough to make an offer on the first one. Be patient. Do your homework. Shop carefully, and look at everything available. Don't allow real estate agents or sellers to rush you for any reason. Wait until your research tells you that you've found the right property. Spend as much time researching an investment as you spent earning the money that you're going to put into it.

Three Methods of Appraising Real Estate

The next thing to consider is the value you're going to put on a piece of property. Three methods are commonly used to evaluate or appraise real estate; you should learn and take all three into consideration when making an offer.

The first is the *market approach*. How much is the house or building selling for per square foot compared to other properties of similar size, condition, amenities and location? Remember this, if a particular feature of a house doesn't add to the value of a house, or if you can't sell the property for more money because of this feature, don't pay extra for it. This rule applies especially to things such as lot size, landscaping, paint, double garage, or swimming pools. These are what are called hygiene factors. If the house has them, they're not worth anything more, but if the house doesn't have them, it is worth less than other, similar houses.

The second method of appraisal is called the *cost approach*, especially the replacement cost. The replacement cost is based on the current cost of construction of a home of similar size and value. What would it cost to build a home similar to this from scratch in today's market? This is a question that you have to answer. Buildings begin deteriorating the day they are completed. They wear out unless they're well-constructed and carefully maintained. When you're evaluating a property for purchase, you must check out both construction and maintenance in detail. Every error of judgment on your part, every factor that you ignore, will end up costing you money, sometimes a lot of money, down the line.

The third method of appraisal is called the *income approach*. This is used for properties that generate income and it's expressed as a rate of return on equity—ROE—or the return on the amount of money that you actually put out of your pocket. This is also known as *return on cash invested*.

Three Methods of Appraising Real Estate

1. Market
2. Cost
3. Income

To use the market approach, you simply compare sales prices—
not listing prices—in the area in recent months on a square-foot basis.
Get a multiple listing book from a friendly realtor and compare the
actual sales prices received for various houses in the neighborhood
that you're looking at. Divide the price by the number of square feet
in the house. Add up twenty or thirty prices, and average them to
get a fairly accurate idea of what the house is worth on a per-square-
foot basis.

To use the cost approach, talk to home builders to find out how
much it would cost to duplicate the same size and quality of building
today on a square-foot basis. Tell them that you're thinking of building a home in a particular community, and ask the approximate
prices that they would charge.

To use the income approach, first calculate the amount at
which you could rent the property in today's market. Then add
up all the expenses associated with owning it, including mortgage
payments, both principal and interest. Second, add up the taxes,
insurance, and all other charges payable that are associated with
ownership, such as the homeowners' associations, condominium
fees, and extra charges for garbage collection or utilities. Third,
add the regular cost of maintenance, such as paint and carpeting.
In rental properties, appliances need to be replaced approximately
every seven years; therefore you must build one seventh of the
cost of new appliances into your calculations as an expense on an
annual basis. Also, deduct any other upkeep expenses for which
you will be responsible. When you have a total of all these, you
deduct this total from the income that the property will generate when rented to a tenant in order to get a net figure. You then
divide your equity or cash investment into the net figure to get
your rate of return.

A residence should rent for 1 percent of its market value per month.

A general rule of residential real estate is that over time a residence should rent for 1 percent of its market value per month, or conversely, it will sell for 100 times its monthly rent. This number holds true until you get into higher-priced homes, which seldom rent for enough even to pay the mortgage and taxes. For this reason, only buy properties in the lower to medium price range.

Making the Offer

When you find a house that is priced right, you make an offer to purchase. The best deal for you is a price no more than 90 percent of market value, with a small or nil cash down payment, a first mortgage of 80 to 90 percent of the purchase price, and the seller agreeing to carry the balance of the purchase price above the mortgage back over five to seven years at an attractive rate of interest.

A good strategy is to put in a lowball offer at first: offer no more than 70 percent of the asking price, even though you know that most houses sell at between 80 and 95 percent of asking price. Sometimes, for reasons you won't know, the seller will accept a ridiculously low offer. Perhaps he's just been transferred. Or maybe the owners are going through a divorce or bankruptcy and need the money immediately.

Always ask why they're selling the house. Sometimes a little information can get you a long way. Before you make an offer, do a detailed calculation of how much you will have to spend to renovate. Use your list of needed repairs and their cost to get the seller to come down in price. The better prepared you are, the more likely you are to drive a good bargain.

Remember, you make your profit by buying right, but you only realize your profit by selling right. When you make a lowball offer, point out each deficiency in the house, and give an estimate of how much it will cost you to repair or remedy it. Often giving good reasons for offering a lower price will cause the seller to come down and accept less than they are asking. Take your time in negotiating on a purchase. Your patience can save you hundreds, if not thousands of dollars.

Again, never allow yourself to be rushed. If you get a complex counteroffer, ask for time to think it over and then sleep on it. Make your decision slowly and carefully.

Repairs and Renovations

Once you've purchased the house, your aim is to fix it up or rent it out as quickly as possible. If you decide to fix it up, you will want to put your money where it goes the furthest in raising the rental or resale value of the house. Here are the key places to spend money in renovating and upgrading.

At the top of the list is good quality paint, using designer or decorator colors. Designer colors are those that go with any type of furniture and with any color scheme. Examples are white, off-white, powder blue, cream, beige, or peach. This type of color is acceptable to almost everyone. No matter what type of furniture a person has, it will fit comfortably into a home that is done in designer colors.

If warranted, paint the outside of the house as well as the inside. New paint can give you a payoff of as much as $5 for every dollar that you spend. This means that the value and resale price of the house will increase by $5 for every dollar that you invest in repainting the house inside and out.

The second place to spend money is on carpets. Again, use designer colors, which are unobtrusive and anyone can be comfortable with. Use better-quality carpet in high traffic areas and cheaper carpets in bedrooms, dens, and basements. Be sure to use neutral tones, and use one color only throughout the entire house. Don't make the mistake of buying batches of carpet at bargain-basement prices and putting different-colored carpeting in different rooms. It looks terrible and ultimately lowers the value of the house, either for resale or rental. Every dollar that you spend on carpet will increase the value of the house by $4: a 400 percent return on your investment.

The third place to invest is in landscaping. Clean up the yard and the outside of the house completely so that it makes a good impression on a person driving up to it for the first time. Real estate agents call this *curb appeal.* Many people have made the first half of their decision to buy or rent before they even come into the house simply by the way it looks on the outside. By investing in landscaping such as flowers and shrubbery, mowing the lawn, and trimming the edges, you can increase the value of the house by as much as $25 for every dollar that you spend.

The fourth place to invest is in fireplaces. According to real estate appraisers, fireplaces add $1.23 in value for every dollar that you spend. This is a good investment, even if you only put in a false gas fireplace.

The fifth place to invest is to add a full bathroom. Another full bathroom increases the value of the house by $1.10 for every dollar that you spend on it.

The sixth area is in new siding, which increases the value of the house dollar for dollar, as well as improving the appearance. Only use siding if you can't achieve the same effect with a good-quality paint.

Everything else that you do in renovating and upgrading the house will return you less than $1 for every dollar that you spend. For example, a minor kitchen remodel which consists of new appliances, new paint and wallpaper, no matter how much it's needed, will give you back only 90 cents in added value for every dollar that you spend. This isn't to say that you shouldn't do it. An ugly kitchen will turn a buyer or a renter off faster than almost anything else. A major kitchen remodel as opposed to a minor kitchen remodel, which includes appliances, paint and wallpaper, plus new cabinets and counters, will return you 89 cents for every dollar of cost. Sometimes you have no choice but to do a major kitchen remodel, but you should know that it is not increasing value; it is merely holding the value of the property.

There are other things that you might do, all of which will add less than 90 cents per dollar that you spend, and sometimes much less. For example, you'll only get 80 cents of increased value for every dollar that you spend on new roofing. On new skylights, 75 cents for each dollar. For adding a wooden deck, 72 cents for every dollar. For installing a swimming pool, you'll only get back 32 cents for every dollar that you pay. Many home buyers consider a pool to be more of a nuisance than an advantage. Whatever you do, don't put one in. If you're buying a house with a pool, don't pay any more for it than you would if it had no pool at all.

To repeat, the most dependable improvements that you can make to add value to a house or apartment in order are paint, carpet, landscaping, fireplaces, bathrooms, and new siding. This is where you should look when appraising a house for opportunities to upgrade and increase value. Of course, if there's repair work to be done on plumbing, electrical or carpentry, you'll have to do these in any case. As I said earlier, make an estimate of all the costs that you feel will be necessary, and then use it as a negotiating tool when you make your offer.

Once you've completed the facelift on the house, inside and out, you are ready to either refinance, sell, or rent it out, and move on to your next project. If you do this twice a year for the next ten years, you'll probably be set for life.

Five Keys to Superleverage

In the final analysis, financial success in real estate comes from leverage or the use of OPM—other people's money—to multiply your return on your equity. However, real wealth creation comes from superleverage, which is based on five keys:

1. The house you are purchasing has a low price relative to the current market, and the lower the better. Any price that has a 20 percent discount or more from similar homes in the same area is the kind of bargain that can help to give you superleverage.

2. Good terms, which means a low interest rate and payments stretched out over several years. In fact, if the key to finding real estate is location, location, location, then the key to buying real estate aside from price is terms, terms, terms. You can pay almost any price within reason if you can have a long enough time to pay it off with low enough interest rates.

3. Get the seller to take back a second mortgage, thereby enabling you to get into the property with little or no cash out of your own pocket.

4. Fast and aggressive upgrading of the property. Time is money. Time is valuable. If you're going to purchase a house to fix up

and rent out, get on with it. Do it fast. Move quickly. The faster you can turn the house around, the more valuable the whole transaction is to you.

5. Refinancing and cashing out—getting your money back and owning the property with no investment at all. Using a simple example, imagine that you have purchased a house for $100,000, and by aggressively upgrading the house, you can increase its value to $120,000. Let us say that you took out an $80,000 first mortgage when you bought it and you made a $20,000 down payment. You could now refinance the house with a $100,000 first mortgage, replacing the $80,000 first mortgage to get your $20,000 back. From that point on, you have the house with no equity investment at all. No matter what you earn from rentals, your rate of return on your investment, which is zero, is astronomical. This is superleverage.

Multifamily Dwellings

Once you get into the swing of buying, fixing, renting, and managing single-family houses, you will be ready to proceed to multifamily dwellings. Everything you have learned with regard to buying one house as an investment holds just as true for a duplex, triplex, four-plex, or an apartment building of any size. The only difference is the scale and the amount of money involved. The only limiting factors are your imagination and your resources. That's why it's better to start small and grow one step at a time, expanding your imagination and your vision of what's possible for you, and, more importantly, increasing your knowledge and experience.

Multiunit Properties

Let's assume that you have gained some experience with single-family homes and you're now ready to move up. How do you determine the right price for an apartment building? The answer is that you use all of the same methods that you have used in evaluating a single-family house. First, you compare the building on the basis of cost per apartment or cost per apartment compared with other buildings of the same size and condition. You use the replacement cost method by finding out what it would cost to build this type of building starting from scratch. You use the market comparison method to find out how much similar apartment buildings are selling for on a per apartment, per square foot basis. You also use the return on equity method, which is perhaps the most important of all in evaluating whether or not this is a good purchase.

Inspect every single unit in the apartment building, taking and keeping careful notes regarding the overall condition, the paint, carpet, and appliances. Be sure to find out how old the appliances are, because they have to be replaced every seven years, and you must consider the amount that they have already depreciated when calculating your offering price. Look at the expenses of operating the building before debt service or mortgage payments. Request complete and accurate numbers, including the bank book, with a listing of all the deposits entered and the checks written.

The cost of operating an apartment building should be 30 percent of the gross or total rents received if the tenants pay the utilities themselves. The expenses of operation should be 40 percent of gross rent if the landlord pays the utilities directly. If either of these figures are off, either high or low, it could mean that the expenses have been understated or there may be potential to reduce expenses and increase cash flow.

When looking at an apartment building for sale, always find out why the purchaser is selling. Get all the information possible about the seller's situation before you make an offer. It could be that he is asking for 20 percent cash down but doesn't need that much cash all at once. Sometimes that much cash all at once would simply have to be paid in higher taxes, so it would be in his best interest to give you better terms to lower the cash down payment and stretch the balance over five to seven years.

In any business, especially in investment, real estate, cash is king. It's not just the most important thing; it's everything. Always think in terms of safeguarding your cash, parting with it slowly, grudgingly, carefully, and not at all if possible.

Every offer to purchase an apartment building should be subject to verification of all revenues and expenses. If the owner is being straight with you, he will show you all records of rental receipts and expenses for the building going back several years. When negotiating with the seller, use all the building's shortcomings and defects to justify a low offer, but be polite, courteous and low-key. Don't reveal your negotiating strategy to anyone, not even the real estate agent. Keep it to yourself. Keep it confidential.

Here's an important point: refuse to allow a real estate agent to carry offers back and forth between you and the seller. Insist on meeting and negotiating directly with the owner. If this isn't possible, you should probably keep on looking for a situation where it is possible. Your personal character and your ability to negotiate in your best interest is one of your most important assets that you have in purchasing apartment property.

Have an engineer check the plumbing, boilers, furnaces, and wiring before you finalize the deal. Have a builder check the structure for soundness. Have an exterminator check for termites or pests of any kind. Remember, you have to approach this property as though you're going to keep it for twenty years. Besides, every flaw that you can find gives you additional ammunition that you can use to get the price down.

Purchasing Commercial Real Estate

Purchasing commercial real estate of any kind requires careful thought and analysis. Just remember that you're buying the property's long-term future earning power, and you must evaluate each opportunity carefully by asking the following questions.

1. How much is it going to cost you in comparison with other properties of equal attractiveness that are for sale in the same area?
2. How much do you get back? What will be your net return on your investment after deducting every conceivable expense?
3. When will you begin to get a return on your money? It's not uncommon for commercial properties to sell at zero cash flow because they're so attractive. An investor will purchase a piece of property where the income from rentals just covers the payments on the mortgages. The investor will do this in anticipation of being able to raise the rents with the passing of time and eventually get back the money in higher cash flow in the next five or ten years. You need to be alert to this tradition in buying and selling apartment properties.
4. How certain is it that your return on an investment will materialize? Every investment contains a certain element of risk

and uncertainty. Real estate entrepreneurs are successful to the degree to which they minimize risk rather than seeking it out. Be very cold-blooded when evaluating how and when you will get your money back once you've put it in.

5. What else can you do with the same amount of money? Where else can you invest the same amount of money to get a similar or greater return? Many people consider this question carefully before selling any investment. If you sell an investment that is giving you a return of 10 percent per annum, you have to decide where else you could invest the money to achieve the same return on investment with the same level of risk.

All this is food for thought if you're planning to become a real estate entrepreneur, starting with single-family homes and moving up to duplexes, triplexes and apartment complexes. In this brief discussion, I've deliberately avoiding issues such as equity buildup, depreciation or amortization rates, the impact of taxes, or discounted cash flows. Only buy a piece of property that makes sense as an investment—never one that only makes sense because of the tax benefits attached to it.

In this chapter, I've covered the basics that you need to know to get started as a real estate entrepreneur. There are many books, courses, and seminars in this subject, and I recommend that you get them, read them, and in the case of the seminars, attend them. As with any business, real estate investment requires an enormous amount of time and energy, dedication, courage, and persistence.

Moreover, you really must enjoy real estate investment if you're going to succeed at it. You must be willing to put your head down for several years, work hard, wrestle with unruly bankers and sellers, negotiate, grind, compromise continually, and fight with difficult tenants who feel that all landlords are fair game. If you persevere in spite of these challenges, one day you could wake up with a substantial portfolio of income producing properties, a healthy cash flow, and financial independence for life.

Major Points

- Real estate is its future earning power.
- Buy homes that need work, fix them up, and either sell them or rent them out for a profit.
- Negative cash flow causes more real estate entrepreneurs to go bankrupt than any other single factor.
- Select tenants very carefully.
- Real estate values increase at approximately double the rate of population growth.
- Invest in a stable community with a solid economic base.
- Never operate on the "greater fool" theory when investing in property.
- Expect to look at 100 houses before you are knowledgeable enough to make an offer on the first one.
- You make your profit by buying right, but you only realize your profit by selling right.
- Cash is king. It's not just the most important thing; it's everything.

7

The How and Why of Money—Yours and Other People's

everage enables you to take advantage of the resources of others to achieve your goals. This concept of leverage—making yourself a multiplication sign, using your talents and abilities to accelerate yourself ahead of others—is really the key concept of achieving success of any kind.

The main type of leverage that I've discussed so far is **OPM**: other people's money. All banking, finance, real estate, and other investment is based on **OPM**. Your ability to use other people's money makes all the difference between accomplishing a little and accomplishing a lot.

However, people are very careful about parting with their money. Commercial bankers are in the business of making good loans, not risky ones. Your friends and associates, who have worked hard for their money, are also extremely cautious about losing it. This is why your credit rating—your proven reliability with regard to money—is something that you need to build up and guard with care throughout your life.

ROI in Its Various Forms

The critical factor in getting the use of other people's money is called ROI or *return on investment*. Every single use of money for investment or development is taken with an eye to ROI. How much money will be put in, and how much will come back as a result? The only reason to borrow money at a specific rate of interest is to earn an even higher rate of interest on the use of that money.

In this sense, money is like a tool, and the rate of interest is a rental rate for the use of the tool. If you can rent money at 10 percent per annum, and you can make it grow at 20 or 30 percent per annum in your own business, you make a profit of 10 percent to 20 percent on the use of the money—the difference between what you pay and what you can earn.

The Various Forms of Return

When you're younger, it' difficult to get a loan to start or build a business. Fortunately, you can use other ROI formulas to increase your value and make it much more likely that you'll get the money you need.

For example, there is *return on inspiration*. This is the extra energy, enthusiasm, and attention that you put into your work when you're inspired about what you're doing. This attitude rapidly brings you to the attention of people who can help you.

There is *return on imagination*. One good idea is all you need to start a fortune. Asking how you could improve what you're doing will often trigger your imagination into coming up with new ideas for cheaper, better, or faster products or services. Many great successes in America began with a person who was continually applying their imagination to find ways to do their work at lower cost or with greater profitability. What ways could you use your imagination more constructively in the work you are doing right now?

There's also *return on intelligence*. Intelligence is a way of acting. Whenever you act in a way that is consistent with achieving your goals and those of your company, you are behaving intelligently. The more you learn about how to be more effective at what you do, the more intelligently you behave, and the more you'll be rewarded. What forms of additional intelligence or knowledge could enable you to contribute more to your current job or customers?

There's also *return on initiative*: the boldness and energy to try new and different things and take on additional responsibilities without being asked to. Very few people have the ability to size up a situation, see what needs to be done, and do it without supervision or direction.

Successful people are motivated by inspiration, imagination, intelligence, and initiative. These four can give you extremely high returns on your investment of time and energy, and they can lead to your becoming a multiplication factor wherever you are placed.

OPE: Other People's Energy

The second kind of leverage that you must have to be successful is OPE: other people's energy. You can accomplish little tasks by yourself, but to accomplish anything big and worthwhile, you'll need to tap into the energies of many different people. Your ability to attract the right kind of people, organize them properly, and get them to produce in excess of the cost of bringing them together is a key skill that will determine your success as much as any other factor.

OPK: Other People's Knowledge

The third common form of leverage is OPK: other people's knowledge. One of the reasons for America's great success is that a new piece of knowledge, no matter where or how generated, can soon be multiplied by hundreds, thousands, even millions of people via books, magazines, television, radio, and of course the Internet. That piece of knowledge can then be used by anyone wherever it is relevant.

The Law of Comparative Advantage

David Ricardo was one of the leading economists in early nineteenth-century England. Ricardo's law, the *law of comparative advantage*, is one of the most important concepts to know in this area. Ignorance of this law causes more unhappiness, frustration, and failure than you could possibly imagine.

You will always be more productive doing the few things that you do the best and which contribute the greatest amount of value to your life and work.

The law of comparative advantage is a mathematical formula that explains the importance and reasoning of using leverage in everything you do. It simply says that you will always be more productive doing the few things that you do the best and which contribute the greatest amount of value to your life and work. At the same time, you must delegate, eliminate, outsource, or deemphasize the activities that do not contribute to your work and life as much as the others.

Ricardo's law is, in a way, the basis of modern management. It is the key to understanding leverage. Like all laws, it's consistent with the law of cause and effect, of sowing and reaping. It says that if you wish to earn $50,000 per year in your field, you have to do $50,000 or more worth of work. You cannot be paid the money you want for very long if you don't earn it. Many people are out on the streets looking for jobs who thought that no one was looking and it didn't really matter if they weren't working hard. Well, someone was watching, and it did matter. People are laid off because, for whatever reason, they are no longer making a contribution that is in excess of their cost to the organization.

For example, there are roughly 250 working days in an average year. If you wanted to earn $50,000 per year, you would divide $50,000 by 250 days to get $200 per day. You would then divide the $200 per day by the 8 hours that you work to reach a figure of $25 per hour as your desired hourly rate. This is your target: if you want to earn $50,000 per year, you must earn $25 per hour. You must do $25 worth of work per hour, 8 hours per day, 250 days per year.

If you want to earn $75,000 per year, you must earn $37.50 per hour, 8 hours per day, 250 days per year. Many people have problems regarding job security and low income because they don't understand this simple point: if you don't earn it, you can't be paid it. If you want to earn $100,000 per year, you must earn $50 per hour. You cannot phone your friends, make your own photocopies, get your car washed, enjoy long, leisurely coffee and lunch breaks, socialize with your friends at work, and end up being paid $100,000 per year.

Here's a simple way to keep yourself on track every hour of every day. Continually ask yourself, would I pay somebody else $50 per hour to do what I'm doing right now? Would you reach into your pocket, take out $50, and give it to someone else to drive around, listen to the radio, read the newspaper over a cup of coffee, or chat with the other people at the office? If you wouldn't pay $50 per hour out of your own pocket for that activity, stop doing it immediately. Discipline yourself to do only those things that pay you as much or more as you wish to earn.

If you start a little earlier, stay a little later, and work a little harder and a little smarter, you can put yourself on the side of the angels. You can give yourself the winning edge. By doing the kind of work that pays the kind of money you want to earn, as sure as God grows little green apples, you will soon be earning the kind of money that you want.

When you're starting off in your career, you earn very little. The value of your contribution is low, so your annual or monthly wage is low. You're usually on your own. Because money is tight, you get into the habit of doing virtually everything for yourself. When I was in my twenties, I did much of my own cooking and most of my own laundry. I did most of the work on my car and was completely responsible for my own housekeeping. If something was torn or if I lost a button, I would get out a needle and thread and repair it myself. I would change my own oil and replace my own transmissions. I would change my own tires when they were flat or worn, and I would wash my own car. When I got my first house, I went out and bought a lawn mower and a bunch of garden tools and spent every Saturday or Sunday mowing my lawn and cleaning up my yard.

When the winter came, I shoveled my own snow. I trimmed my own sidewalks, pruned my own trees; inside, I moved my own furniture and carried my own boxes.

I did this for many years. When I got married and we got a house and then another house, I felt very responsible. Even though I was working harder and harder at my job and earning more money, I still felt that I had a duty to get all these things done.

One Saturday afternoon, after I had spent three hours in the hot sun mowing my yard and cleaning up the garden, I was sitting in the shade resting when my wife, Barbara, came up to me and sat down. She said that we needed to hire someone to mow the lawn and take care of the yard.

"Wait a minute," I said, "what's wrong with the way I'm doing it right now?"

She said something I'll never forget, and which is relevant to you as well: "Brian, you can no longer afford to mow your own lawn. Your time is simply too valuable to be spent working in the yard. It would be better if you just sat and rested or spent time with the children than working at something that we could get done for a few dollars an hour."

This was a hard thing for me to accept at first, but I immediately recognized that she was right. I was locked in an old paradigm, an old rut, an old way of doing things. The only way to move ahead was to let go of some of the old things I was doing so I could have more time and energy for new possibilities.

Managing yourself enables you to get far more output per units of input.

Managing yourself enables you to get far more output per units of input. It enables you to maximize your talents, abilities, and resources to give you the highest return on energy—physical, emotional, and mental—that is possible for you. Self-management is a key skill that is practiced by all high-achieving men and women.

Managing Others

The natural extension of self-management is the management of others. Management has been defined as getting results through others. You always have a choice: you can do the job yourself, or you can get someone else to do it. If you do the job yourself, you have the power of one person working. If you get the job done through someone or several others, you have the power of many working for you. Your success depends on utilizing the power of many others and coordinating their activities so that your results greatly exceed what you could get working by yourself.

Perhaps the greatest breakthrough in the increase of production was the systematic division of labor into specialized tasks. That's what you have to do. Since any result requires completion of a large number of tasks, you have to think through what these tasks are. Then you must decide which of them you absolutely must do yourself and which can be done by others. Your job is not to do the whole task, but to coordinate the activities of other people so that the whole task gets done. This is the great art and science of management, and it is the ultimate in leveraging yourself for maximum achievement.

When you start off at any job or in any new business, you have to learn from the ground up. You have to pay your dues. You have to do all the little jobs as well as the big jobs. When I was starting off, I typed my own letters, stapled my own papers, bought my own paper clips, stamped my own letters, and cleaned my own floor. As I mastered the basic tasks and became busier and more successful,

I was able to hire other people, first part-time and then full-time, to do the things that I had already mastered and which were no longer good uses of my time.

Many people make the mistake of wanting to start at the top.

It will probably be the same for you. Many people make the mistake of wanting to start at the top. They consider themselves to be too good to roll up their sleeves and do the heavy lifting that's required at the beginning. They want to give orders to other people to do things that they don't understand how to do themselves. They don't realize that a tall building has a deep foundation. A great career is built on a solid foundation of complete mastery of the basic tasks.

The starting point of the art of management is simple. It's the determination of a business objective that requires more energy and efforts than are possessed by any one person. At this point, the science of management clicks in. It becomes necessary to involve other people in the process. At this point, you begin to demonstrate one of the greatest arts of Western civilization: modern management.

No matter how complicated management responsibilities or tasks become, they always boil down to answering two questions: What are we trying to do? And how are we trying to do it? Whenever you're in doubt for any reason, stop the clock, drop the flag, and ask these questions. Answering them accurately is the starting point and foundation of managerial effectiveness.

Functions of Management

The art, science, and process of management do not necessarily come naturally. Management must be learned, studied, and practiced.

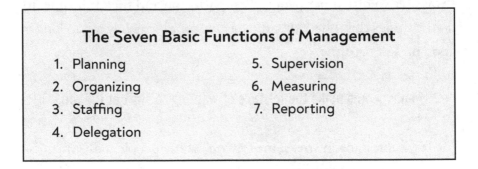

The Seven Basic Functions of Management

1. Planning
2. Organizing
3. Staffing
4. Delegation
5. Supervision
6. Measuring
7. Reporting

There are hundreds of business schools and courses and thousands of books, articles, and magazines on management. Some of the best work on the subject has been done in the last few years. From the time when you begin your career until the day you retire, you should be drinking in management material the way you breathe in oxygen. Learning about being more effective as a manager should be a regular part of your entire work life. Take courses, read books, and listen to audio material. Sometimes just one little idea can be the key to the situation you're facing. Having that bit of knowledge can enable you to achieve great success and save you years of hard work.

There are seven basic functions that apply to both self-management and the management of others:

1. Planning
2. Organizing
3. Staffing
4. Delegation
5. Supervision
6. Measuring
7. Reporting

These are the big seven. Whether you manage one person or a thousand, you engage in these seven continually.

Planning

The first function of management is planning. It is an essential management skill. Planning is setting goals and objectives. It's determining where you want to go and how you're going to get there. Planning entails the ability to articulate the goals clearly, write them down, and make them measurable. Clarity is essential.

The critical activity of planning is the definition of the ideal end state.

Many present-day problems for companies and managers arise from the fact that they do little or no planning. Their goals are fuzzy or unclear. Perhaps 80 to 90 percent of companies today are immersed in operating rather than managing. They are walking forward with their eyes on the ground in front of them rather than on the horizon ahead of them. They are so caught up in day-to-day activities that they seldom take the time to ask, "What exactly are we trying to accomplish? What are our real long-term goals?"

The critical activity of planning is the definition of the ideal end state. What results are you trying to achieve? What outcomes do you desire? If you achieved your goals exactly as you want, what would they look like? How would you be able to tell that you achieved them successfully? It's often been said that the devil is in the details. Planning roots out flaws that can be extremely costly later.

Organizing

The second function of management is *organizing*. Once you've decided what you want to accomplish, you make a list of all of the resources that you require to achieve your goal. If you want to build a business, achieve a certain level of sales, produce a product, or reorganize a department, first you think about what you will need to do the job in an excellent fashion. There's a saying in warfare that amateurs talk strategy, while professionals talk logistics. This means that having great goals and objectives is a wonderful thing, but they're only a prelude to the real work. The real work is sitting down, thinking through, and acquiring the people, skills, money, and material resources you need to do the job well.

Organizing is very much like building a bridge. You want to get from one side to the other. To do that, you need to assemble all of the materials for its construction. There's no point beginning construction with insufficient materials.

If you're not capable of managing a project, you must always work under someone else who is.

What kind of talents and skills will you need to achieve your goals and objectives? How much will it cost? Where will the money come from? How long will it take? What can go wrong? Your ability to plan a multitask job—one that will require completion of several smaller jobs—is one of the most important skills that you can ever develop. In fact, if you're not capable of managing a project, you must always work under someone else who is.

Managing a project is very much like achieving a goal: You make a list of activities, and you organize the activities in terms of priorities. You then organize the activities in terms of time and sequence, and you start working on your plan.

Staffing

The third function of management is *staffing*: carefully selecting the members of your team. It includes interviewing and selecting the men and women with the skills to achieve the goals and objectives for which you are responsible. This is one of the most important skills of management. It's been said that 95 percent of success in business lies in this selection process.

To paraphrase an old proverb, if you select in haste, you will repent at leisure. Hire people carefully, hire them slowly, check their references thoroughly, and always trust your gut feeling. Almost all problems in business are people problems, which often go back to mistakes that were made in selection in the first place.

Delegation

The fourth function of management is *delegation*. This is the key skill to multiply yourself and your abilities. It is perhaps the most important technique of management. All personal effectiveness in managerial roles depends on your ability to pick the right people, put them in the right places, and then ensure that they get the job done on schedule. Delegation enables you to leverage yourself and get an enormous amount of work done through the organization, deployment, and allocation of human resources.

When delegating, think through the job or task to be done. If you're going to hire someone on the outside to perform that service, think it through carefully and be very selective. If you're going to hire an employee or assign a responsibility to someone who works for you, remember that delegation is not abdication: you are still accountable. The success or failure of this delegatee is your success or failure as well. Don't rush. Take your time. Be patient. Take all the time necessary to think it through.

When delegating, don't look for or expect perfection. If another person can do the job 70 percent as well as you, it's probably all right, unless the performance of the job is critical to many other things. In delegating, the only real predictor of future performance is past performance. It's not with the person who thinks they can do but what they have done in the past. This is not to say that a person can't learn and grow with new responsibilities, but you must carefully think through how the individual has performed with previous responsibilities before delegating anything important.

When you delegate a task, give authority commensurate with responsibility. Give the person the time and resources necessary to do the job properly. Set deadlines on every task that you delegate. If it's a large task to be done over an extended period of time, set subdeadlines as well.

In delegating, remember all the variations of Murphy's law: whatever can go wrong will go wrong at the worst possible time and will cost the greatest amount of money. Whenever I delegate a task, I have the other person write it down in front of me and then read it back. At least 50 percent of cases, even the most sincere and intelligent person gets it wrong. They hear something you didn't say and they don't hear something you did say. Take the time to make sure that the other person knows exactly what is to be done, how it will be measured, and when it is to be completed.

If you have any doubt about understanding, write it in a brief memo and send it to the person in written form. Often that simple act will save you many hours of frustration and enormous sums of money.

Supervision

The fifth function of management is *supervision*. The best form of supervision follows accurate and clear delegation: you check with the other person on a regular basis to make sure they're on track with the job. Whenever possible, set up a regular schedule of meetings to review progress. Watch for unexpected problems and delays. Be sensitive to the fact that the job may be over the employee's head. Be prepared to step in to help or get other resources so that they can stay on schedule.

For example, the controller for my corporation is a very fine and capable woman. However, as our company grew, her responsibilities and activities increased dramatically. Soon she was coming in early and staying later every day. It was obvious that it was wearing her down, but she felt so responsible for getting the accounting done on time that she just kept working harder and harder. Finally, I stepped in and insisted that she get additional help. She was reluctant, but finally went along. We soon hired a full-time bookkeeper who was able to do much of the basic accounting so that my controller could dedicate herself to the few financial statements that were most important. Soon she began to relax and get back to her old self.

The basic rule of supervision is to inspect what you expect.

The basic rule of supervision is to inspect what you expect. This doesn't mean that continually looking over people's shoulders. It simply means checking regularly to see how things are going. Studies show that employees consider a task to be important to the degree that the boss asks about it on a regular basis. Your job is always to know the status of the critical tasks for which you're responsible. This requires that you ask and receive accurate answers and have subordinates account for deadlines. It is essential to resist the temptation toward reverse or upward delegation: when the employee delegates the task back to you, often claiming to be too busy or unskilled or unsure. They ask if you would handle this task for them: "Would you phone such and such a person or get them such and such a piece of information?" "Perhaps you could write a letter or a proposal." In many cases they come to you with a problem and ask if you could think it through and come up with a solution for them. Then away they go—free at last. You now have the job. It's back on your lap.

Many managers find themselves working long into the evening on tasks they had originally assigned to other people, but which were somehow reverse-delegated back to them. This sort of thing happens in your private life as well: people are always trying to get you to do work they should be doing. The key question you always have to ask, is, who is getting paid to do this job? That's the person who's responsible for the work. Refuse to take it back.

Measuring

The sixth function of management is *measuring*. In measuring the performance of another person, you need objective criteria; you need standards of performance; you need standards of quality or output. You need to agree in advance what you want done and how you will know it was done to an acceptable level. It's not enough to tell a person to go out and make sales: you must tell them that you want and expect a certain level of sales within a certain time period. Numbers don't lie. Get agreement on how success will be measured in advance, and use the numbers objectively to assess how well the person has done the job. The better use you make of numbers, the less likely it is that you will have to get involved in personalities when problems arise. Instead of saying, "You, you, you," you can simply refer to the agreed-upon measurement criteria and focus the discussion on the job rather than on the person.

Reporting and Surprises

The seventh function of management is *reporting*. Whoever you are, you have to report to someone. When you work for a company, you have to report to your superior on a regular basis. Even if you are a senior manager with an extensive staff, there is always someone above you to whom you have to report results. Your ability to report in a timely, accurate fashion is a real measure of how competent and capable you are. The people above you don't like being left in the dark. There's one thing that they like even less, and that is surprises. That's because surprises are very seldom positive. If you anticipate a problem of any kind, report it in advance so that there is no shock when it does happen.

Surprises are seldom positive.

At a company that I was consulting with recently, the budget projections showed that there was one division of the company that was making $10 million of annual sales and generating $4 million in profit. The total profits of the whole company for the year were $8 million. However, as they installed a new computer system, it became clear to the executive in charge that the entire way of calculating sales was messed up. It turned out that they weren't making $10 million worth of sales at all. They were only making $5 million in sales, and they had been double-counting the sales for the last year. They weren't making $4 million in profits. They were losing more than $1 million every twelve-month period.

When the president of the company finally got the bad news, the senior executive in charge was fired, and the department was cleared out and completely reorganized. If the news had been relayed to the president as soon as the first signs of problems occurred, it might have led to a completely different outcome.

By the way, even if you own your own company, you still have to report to your bankers, shareholders, staff, customers, and everyone else whose approval or disapproval affects the health of your business. Reporting is a discipline. The very exercise of preparing accurate analysis and reports helps you to understand it better and perform more effectively. The best businesspeople I have met are extremely knowledgeable and precise about the results of their activities. They measure them continually.

Leadership in Action

Management is leadership in action. Your ability to manage human and material resources to get things done through others—to multiply your talents and abilities with other people's money, efforts, and knowledge—is the true demonstration of leadership. The better at it you become, the more you will accomplish in a short time. There's an old saying: "There are no bad soldiers under a good officer."

This is a big subject, but let it be sufficient to say that the people around you are very much a reflection of your own talents and abilities. Large, sophisticated companies have competent, talented executives and staff. Young, inexperienced entrepreneurial ventures have inexperienced and often incompetent people. The manager or leader sets the standard. No one in the organization will be better than he or she is. Your job as a manager is to get continually better so that the people you attract to you will be better as well.

Your ability to budget, make projections, plan, organize, and meet your numbers is the measure of your competence as a manager. The basic formula for management is *talent times relationships equals productivity*, or T x R = P. Your talents, skills, abilities and experience, multiplied by the number of people that you can affect or control, equals the quantity and quality of what you produce. It determines your rewards and your position in life. It determines how high you fly and how far you go.

In the biblical parable, the master says, "Well done, thou good and faithful servant: thou hast been faithful over a few things, I will make thee ruler over many things" (Matthew 25:21). If you do small jobs well, you will soon be given bigger and bigger jobs to manage. In everything you do, your job is to become an excellent manager, become a multiplication sign, leverage yourself and use your talents to accelerate the speed at which you achieve results. Your skill as a manager will determine your level of success and achievement as much as any other skill you could learn in your career.

Ten Commandments for Success

There is virtually nothing that you cannot do if you are willing to, first, learn what you need to know, and second, keep at it long and hard enough until you finally win through.

In this final section, I'm going to give you a track to run on. It's a summary of many previous concepts, and you may refer back to this section whenever you feel frustrated or progress seems to be too slow. These ideas will enable you to refocus your efforts and get back

---

Ten Commandments for Success

1. Set clear goals, and plan accordingly.
2. Develop a success mentality.
3. Be result-oriented and action-oriented.
4. Concentrate your powers.
5. Commit to excellence.
6. Respect your money.
7. Develop a wealthy mindset.
8. Develop a philosophy of time management.
9. Guard your relationships.
10. Live and act with courage.

---

onto the high road. I could call these the "Ten Commandments for Maximum Performance."

Set Clear Goals

The first commandment is to set clear, specific written goals for every area of your life. In business, this is called a business plan. Your business plan for your financial or your personal life must include everything that you want to accomplish and all of the steps you're going to have to take to attain each of your major objectives.

Develop a clear goal and an action plan for the achieving financial independence, including how much you want, what you're going to do to achieve it, and when you're going to reach your financial goals.

Similarly, you need clear goals for your family and your relationships. It is your duty to decide what kind of life you want to live with the people who are most important to you. What do you want to do for and with them? In what time period? How do you want them to think about you and talk about you? What do you need to do on a daily and weekly basis to achieve and maintain the quality of relationships that you desire?

You need goals for your health, including how much you want to weigh and how fit you intend to be. You need a plan for the way you eat and an exercise program to keep you at the maximum level of fitness. You need to plan and program rest and recreation into your life to ensure that you're physically capable of maximum performance in every area of your life.

You need business and career goals as well. You need to identify the steps that you must take and the goals you must achieve to rise to the top in your field.

You need personal and professional development goals. You need a plan for continuously upgrading your skills and abilities and making yourself more competent and valuable. One of the best uses of your time is to become better at the most important tasks that you perform.

Finally, you need spiritual goals: goals for inner development. You know that peace of mind is the highest human good, and your primary responsibility to yourself is to achieve and maintain your own peace of mind.

One way to set and achieve goals is to plan strategically. Work back from your goal to the present moment. Break your larger goals down into subgoals. Break your three- to five-year goals down into six-month, three-month, and one-month goals. Keep your thoughts clearly on where you want to be in the future. Then organize and adjust your daily activities so that every step you take is moving you in that direction.

Review your goals and plans continually. No plan is ever perfect the first time it's put on paper. It will contain numerous defects. There's nothing wrong with that, as long as you're ready to revise, modify, and adapt your plans as you get newer and better information. Remain flexible: it's the most essential quality for success in a rapidly changing, dynamic economy.

To clarify your thoughts, always think on paper. Crystallize your goals and plans by writing and rewriting them over and over again.

High achievers are continual planners. They work with a pad and a pen, making lists, analyzing the results, and revising their plans all the time.

One key to strategic thinking is to carefully consider the consequences of each decision and action in advance. What is likely to happen if you decide to do one thing or another? What will be the primary consequences? What will be the secondary consequences? How are other people likely to react if you choose a particular course of action?

Success means never relying on luck. Indeed action without thinking is the cause of every failure. When you precede every decision and action by careful thought, when you practice thoughtfulness on a regular basis, you will be much more likely to move steadily toward your goals.

Develop a Success Mentality

The second commandment for lifelong success is to develop a success mentality and an unshakable, positive mental attitude. Your thoughts become your realities, so you owe it to yourself to keep your thoughts consistently positive.

Begin by seeing yourself as the president and chief executive officer of your own personal services corporation. Think about yourself as a senior executive. Walk, talk and treat other people as though you were a very important person, because you are: you are the most important person in your world. With the tools that I've been describing, you're on your way to becoming an exceptional human being. Even if you work for another company, treat the company as though it belongs to you. Put your whole heart into your work, and be the kind of person that others look to as an example of the ideal employee.

Think of yourself as a role model for others, your coworkers, and members of your family. Think and speak positively and constructively about other people and situations all the time. Self-mastery and self-control begin with your thoughts and words. Watch what you say: whatever you express is impressed back into your own subconscious mind and will arise again to have a positive or negative effect on your life and relationships.

Keep your vision before you. Think about your goals, ideals, values, and hopes as you go through the day. All improvement in your life begins with an improvement in your mental pictures. There's a one-to-one relationship between how clearly you see your goals in your mind and how rapidly they materialize in your reality. If you practice visualizing your goals repeatedly, eventually they become sharper and more vivid and begin to take on tangible form.

Maintain an attitude of complete faith and confidence that you will achieve what you are meant to achieve when you are ready to achieve it. The law of sowing and reaping works 100 percent of the time. When you have sowed enough, you will reap the abundant harvest.

Be Result-Oriented

The third commandment is to be result-oriented and action-oriented. Intense result orientation is the key to peak performance and the achievement of results of superior quality and quantity. High-performing men and women get more and better results than average and mediocre performers.

Work on your key result areas all the time. If you work for a company, continually ask yourself, "Why am I on the payroll?" What specific, measurable results have you been hired to accomplish? Of all the results that you could be getting with your time and talents, which ones can have the greatest positive impact on your company and career? What is the strategic key to your job or your business?

In every job, every problem, every situation, there is a key that unlocks the future—a key that leads to the solution. In every career, there is a key skill or performance area that leads to rapid advancement. In every business, there's a key element that determines the success and profitability of the enterprise. As you become a more skillful thinker, you will develop this success quality, this ability to look through the situation to the critical element that determines success and failure.

In your company and in your job, ask, "What can I, and only I, do that, if done well, will make an important contribution?" There's always one thing that you can do, which, if you do it in a superior fashion, will have more of an impact on your job success than any other. The smartest men and women ask the right questions. When you continually ask yourself these difficult questions, the answers will enable you to focus on the one or two things that you should be doing that are more important to you and your company than anything else.

Concentrate Your Powers

The fourth commandment for great success is simply concentrate your powers with single-minded intensity of purpose. This commandment alone will enable you to increase if not eventually double your productivity. All high-performing men and women concentrate single-mindedly on one thing—the most important thing—and stay with it until it's finished. Probably the single most important reason for failure and underachievement is the inability to concentrate—the inability to develop and maintain a high level of intensity toward the achievement of your goals.

To help you concentrate your powers, work from a list, a plan, a written blueprint for your activities. Every weekend, sit down and plan out your most important activities for the coming week. Every evening, review your progress for the day and make a written plan for the day ahead. When you write out clearly what you intend to do, you're much more likely to stick to your program than if you attempt to make it up as you go along.

Use the 80-20 rule on everything. Set your priorities based on the maximum positive impact that each activity can have on your future. This will invariably be the highest value use of your time. You have tremendous strengths, talents, and abilities, but you can only use them when you develop the habit of concentrating your powers on the most valuable use of your time every hour of every day.

Commit to Excellence

The fifth commandment for getting onto the high road is to commit to excellence in your field. Everyone who enjoys financial and personal success is recognized as being among the leaders in their field. Excellence is always a journey, never a destination. It's a trip that you set out on when you decide that you're going all the way to the top. You never stop traveling forward; you become better and better until you retire and leave the field.

Begin your journey toward excellence by defining the success factors in your work or business. There are usually five or six reasons for success in any area of endeavor. If you're in sales, these factors could be:

- Prospecting
- Getting appointments
- Presenting
- Answering objections
- Closing
- Following up to ensure satisfaction and referrals

If you're running a business, your success factors could be:

- The quality of your products or services
- The effectiveness of your advertising
- The strength of your sales efforts
- The accuracy of your financial controls and systems
- Your ability to attract the right people
- Your ability to arrange for the money that you need

In every profession, success rests upon one or more of these or similar factors. A weakness in even one area can be fatal.

Once you've identified the success factors in your field, organize them in order of importance. You may be strong in three or four and weak in one or two. In any case, once you've identified these factors, your job is to commit yourself to becoming excellent in each of them one at a time, beginning with the most pressing. Often improvements in just one area can lead to dramatic improvements in your overall results.

The second part of this commandment—committing to excellence—is to do what you love to do, what you most enjoy. Look for work that is intrinsically motivating. This is work that, because of its very nature, you are interested in and happy about. Doing what you love to do is one of the most important rules for success in any job or any business. Become brilliant on the basics. Men and women who excel and achieve are always excellent at the little things. The British historian Thomas Carlyle once wrote, "Genius is an infinite capacity for taking pains."

People who aspire to the heights are never too busy to learn and pay attention to every detail of the business. Sometimes ignoring an almost insignificant factor can lead to the failure of the entire enterprise. Small differences in your competence, in the basics, in the key areas of your work can yield huge differences in results. Always aim for quality of work over quantity. Always take the time to do the job well. Someone once said that there's never enough time to do it right, but there always seems to be enough time to do it over. Quality work is remembered long after speed has been forgotten. In fact, getting a reputation for doing quality work will do as much to advance your career and your income as much as anything else.

Respect Your Money

The sixth commandment for maximum performance is: respect your money, and it will respect you. A positive and constructive attitude toward money and financial accumulation is essential if you're going to make the kind of money that you desire. Since it's your actions that count, you can often tell how you feel about money by the way you handle it. People who are successful with money usually keep their cash folded neatly and organized sequentially in their pocket, wallet, or purse. They keep their checkbooks current and balanced, with each deposit and withdrawal noted. At any given time, they can give you a pretty accurate statement of their financial resources. On the other hand, people who don't respect money tend to have cash jumbled up in their pockets or their purse, their checkbooks are a mess, and the only thing they know for sure about their financial status is that it is worrisome and confused.

Which of these two pictures best describes you? Start respecting your money by working from a written budget in your work, business, and personal life. Set a series of clear, written financial goals and then make plans to accomplish them through systematic financial accumulation. Once you've set a budget, discipline yourself to stick to it. If you allocate yourself a certain amount for rent, transportation, clothing, food, dining out, and so on, make a note of each expenditure and then use your willpower to stay within your own constraints. In a way, a financial budget is a planning tool for long-term monetary success. When you write something down, it becomes a promise to yourself. How well you keep this promise is a measure of your own integrity, and it will affect your self-esteem— your reputation with yourself. People who are disciplined and orderly with regard to their finances tend to be disciplined and orderly with regard to other things as well.

In any case, you seldom find a person who has achieved financial independence who is sloppy and casual about money. Begin today to save 10 percent of your net income as you earn it. Pay yourself first, put the money away, and allow it to grow through compound interest. Take full advantage of an IRA, Keogh, of 401(k) plan, which allows you to accumulate money on a tax-free basis. Your savings will translate into both freedom and opportunity. When you have enough money in the bank to cover two or three months of expenses, you have the freedom to decide where you will work and what you will do. You don't have to put up with a situation that you don't enjoy or doesn't make you happy.

Money in the bank also represents opportunity. Very often when your mind is magnetized with a desire for financial independence, you will attract investment and business opportunities that you can only take advantage of because you have your savings put away.

The opposite of financial freedom is being a financial slave: being enslaved to your bills and to your financial responsibilities. When you don't have money in the bank, you tend to be preoccupied with money most of the time, and this is not a good way to live.

Finally with regard to respecting your money, the first part of financial success is to earn the money, and the second part is to hold on to it. As we've seen, one multimillionaire set out his rules for financial accumulation: "I have just two rules: The first rule is don't lose money. The second rule is, whenever you're tempted, refer back to rule number one."

Develop a Wealthy Mindset

The seventh commandment for high achievement is become wealthy by developing a wealthy mindset. While you can achieve financial independence by saving 10 percent of your income throughout your working life and allowing it to compound, you can become wealthy far faster by developing a wealth-oriented attitude. Your attitude is your approach to matters and situations that involve money. It's the way you view your world in terms of wealth creation.

A good rule to remember is that wealth is income from other sources. You're not wealthy because you make a lot of money; you're wealthy when you have money that comes in whether you work or not. Your first job in financial accumulation is to invest your money in assets that appreciate and yield positive cash flow. Assets that appreciate, like homes, land, and commercial buildings are very different from assets that depreciate, such as cars, boats, and motor homes.

Both wealth and profit come from adding value, from finding ways to increase the value of a product or service by doing something to it. If you assemble raw materials and manufacture a product that you can sell for substantially more than the cost of the raw materials and the labor, you have added value. If you get the right to sell a product or service and you go out and show a customer how the product or service can benefit him or her, you are adding value. Before you do anything involving your hard-earned money, study and learn every detail of the business or the investment. Take nothing on faith. Be extremely cautious. Remember the old saying: "When a man with money meets a man with experience, the man with the experience is going to end up with the money, and the man with the money is going to end up with the experience."

Develop a Philosophy of Time Management

The eighth commandment for great success is develop a philosophy of time management. Time is the one indispensable and irretrievable resource of achievement and financial accumulation. Your attitude toward time—how you think about it as a fundamental part of your life—will tell a lot about how well you do. Here are four ideas that will help you in developing a philosophy of time management.

First, take the long view. Develop a long-term time perspective. Think about what you are doing, and evaluate your decisions and actions based on their likely impact on your life five and ten years from now.

Second, take the short view. Live your life minute by minute. Remember that in the final analysis, the only time that you will ever have is now. A great day, a great week, a great year, and a great lifetime are nothing more or less than a series of excellent moments.

Third, treat your time like money: spend it carefully. It's really all that you have to sell. This means that when you're working, you can't spend your time socializing, dropping off your dry cleaning, picking up your groceries, or drinking coffee. You must work all the time you work.

Do it now is the best motto.

Fourth, you must develop a sense of urgency. *Do it now* is the best motto to learn and internalize. Develop the habit of moving fast on opportunities and responsibilities. Get on with it. Don't delay. Success is a numbers game. The more things you try in a given period of time, the more likely you are to succeed. The faster you work, the more energy you have, and the harder you work, the luckier you get. Develop a sense of urgency. Develop a reputation for speed and dependability. Become known as the person who, when somebody wants something done fast, they give it to you. This habit alone will open more doors for you than you can presently imagine.

Guard Your Relationships

The ninth commandment for success and high achievement is to guard the quality of your relationships with others. More than 85 percent of all the happiness that you will ever enjoy will come from your relationships with other people. If success can be measured in terms of peace of mind and loving relationships, then there's probably nothing that is more important in both the long and short term than to safeguard your relationships and place their health above all other considerations.

Treat everyone, starting at home, like a million-dollar customer. Treat the members of your family as though they were worth a fortune to you. Because when you think about it, they certainly are. You would probably trade everything in the world for the health and well-being of the people who are closest to you. Yet you often think little of treating them with rudeness or indifference when you're tired or irritable. The spiritual leader Emmet Fox once said if you must be rude, be rude to strangers, but save your company manners for your family.

Guard your integrity as a sacred thing. Your integrity and your character form the foundation for all your relationships. The way you get along with other people on the outside reflects how you're getting along with yourself on the inside. When you develop the high qualities of character and integrity, you'll find that your relationships go much more smoothly. More people will want to do business with you and provide you with resources.

Practice the Golden Rule with everyone, especially those who don't practice it themselves. Always do unto others as you would have them do unto you. Never let anyone else's poor behavior or lack of ethics be an excuse for compromising your standards. If people are rude, treat them with charity. If people are unethical, treat them with care. But never allow yourself to descend to their level.

Activate the law of reciprocity by always looking for opportunities to do things for others. Become known as a go-giver as well as a go-getter. Every time that you do a favor or kindness for someone else, you develop within that person a propensity to return the favor to you. This is one of the most powerful of all subconscious influences: the desire to free oneself from obligation when one receives a favor. You can trigger this law of reciprocity in others by always looking for opportunities to put in more than you take out.

Finally, always be courteous and considerate with others, even those who are rude and inconsiderate. Remember, everyone you meet is carrying a heavy load. They all have problems that are weighing down on their hearts and souls, and they're often unaware of the effect of their behavior on others.

Courage: The Foremost Virtue

The tenth commandment for great success is that courage is the foremost of the virtues, because your very success depends upon it. Courage underlies and supports all other beneficial qualities. Dare to go forward. The future belongs to the risk takers, not the security seekers. The future belongs to those rare few who dare to move out of their comfort zones into areas of uncertainty and challenge. One of the best pieces of advice I have ever heard was, "Act boldly, and unseen forces will come to your aid." Whenever you decide to act boldly, to dare to go forward into the unknown, it seems that all kinds of natural forces rise up to help and support you.

Do the thing you fear, and the death of fear is certain.

Overcome the fear of failure that holds most people back by confronting your fears. Do the thing you fear, and the death of fear is certain. Make it a lifelong habit to identify your fears; then turn toward them, confronting them squarely and moving into them rather than moving away. Master your fears, especially your worries, by always asking, "What's the worst possible thing that can happen to me if I go ahead?" Whenever you analyze a worrisome situation by asking this question, your worry seems to dissipate almost immediately. Then go to work with all of your energy and intelligence to make sure that the worst possible thing doesn't happen.

The only real antidote to fear and worry is positive, constructive action toward a predetermined goal. Once you've identified the worst possible outcome, ask yourself, what would be the ideal solution to this difficulty? Then go to work on bringing that solution into reality. It's been well said that if you aim for the moon, you may not hit it, but you will at least hit the stars.

Everyone is afraid of something. The brave person is not the one who has no fear, but the one who acts in spite of his or her fear. It's normal and natural to be uneasy about change or something new and different. But that's not a sufficient excuse for staying in the same place or resisting change when it comes along.

The most important part of acting bravely in the face of uncertainty is that courageous actions develop the habit of courage. If you back away from the things that you fear, you develop the habit of cowardice, of continually backing away. Over time, you will tend to act more and more in accordance with whichever habit you develop. For your own sake and for the sake of your future, you owe it to

---

Seven Principles for Positive Thinking

1. You get not what you want in life, but what you deserve.
2. Your rewards will always be equal to the value of your service.
3. You will always be paid in direct proportion to what you do, how well you do it, and the difficulty of replacing you.
4. You are being paid today exactly what you're worth.
5. The quality of your life will be determined by the depth of your commitment to excellence.
6. Your situation today is exactly what you need right now.
7. Your success will be determined by what you do *after* you've done what you're required to do.

---

yourself to develop the habit of unshakable courage, to dare to go forward. When you act boldly, unseen forces will come to your aid.

Seven Principles for Positive Thinking

Finally, here are seven principles for positive, constructive, and accurate thinking. These principles are based on universal laws, and they explain success and failure as well as any other principles you'll ever learn.

1. You get not what you want in life, but what you deserve or what you earn. Desiring something is not enough. The law of cause and effect says that you first must put in the cause if you desire to enjoy the effect. The law of sowing and reaping says that you first must plant the crop if you wish to harvest it. You will always get what you deserve, and you are getting exactly what you deserve right now. Fortunately, because you can increase the quality and

quantity of your efforts, you can build yourself up to the point where you deserve far more. Then you'll reap a different crop again, exactly as you deserve, with your new talents and abilities.

2. Your rewards will always be equal to the value of your service to others. Our economy is a service economy: we're rewarded by others, our boss, and our customers in direct proportion to the value that they place on our services to them. If you wish to increase the quantity of your rewards, you only need to increase the quality and quantity of your service.

   The house you live in and the car you drive are simply a measure of how valuable your fellow men and women as customers consider your services to be. This doesn't mean that you're not a valuable person. It simply means that people are only willing to pay for certain things in certain amounts, and the amount that they're willing to pay you today represents their fair estimate of the value of what you're now doing for them.

3. You will always be paid in direct proportion to what you do, how well you do it, and the difficulty of replacing you. If you're not happy with the amount that you're earning, you can always do one of three things: (1) you can do something different, (2) you can get better at what you're doing already, or (3) you can do what you're doing somewhere else, where it's possible for you to be paid more.

   In every case, the difficulty of replacing you will have a major impact on how much you receive. That's why they say that it's never crowded at the top. People who are known for high-quality work and companies that are known for high-quality products and services are always the highest-paid and most profitable in their fields.

4. You are being paid today exactly what you're worth: no more and no less. What you are worth today is the sum total result of all of your education and experience combined with how you're applying it to get results for others. Because of the law of cause and effect, you can never take more out of the universe than you put into it. In the long run, you can never be paid more than your worth. Your job is to increase the value of what you do so that you are worth more. In this way you will attract the people and situations that will enable you to be paid at your new level of worth.

5. The quality of your life will be determined by the depth of your commitment to excellence, no matter what your chosen field. The quality of your life, your self-esteem and your self-respect, the esteem and regard in which you're held by others, and the quality and the quantity of the rewards that you receive from your work will all be determined by how well you do what you do. Your commitment to excellence, to be the best, will move you upward and onward faster than any other decision that you could ever make.

6. Your situation today is exactly what you need right now for your own growth and development. The situation that you find yourself in, with all of your problems and difficulties, has been sent to you at this moment to teach you what you need to learn. Difficulties come not to obstruct, but to instruct. Your job is to look into your situation and determine what you're meant to learn as a result of where you find yourself today. Every situation can be a positive situation if viewed as an opportunity for growth and self-mastery. Wherever you are and whatever you're doing, it is exactly what you need at this moment to continue your growth and evolution.

7. Your success will be determined by what you do *after* you've done what you're required to do. If you only do what's expected of you, you can never be paid any more than you're earning

now. But if you put in more than you take out, if you go the extra mile, if you make a habit of exceeding the expectations of your boss and your customers, you will put yourself on the side of the angels. In his essay "Compensation," Ralph Waldo Emerson writes, "If you serve an ungrateful master, serve him the more. Put God in your debt. Every stroke shall be repaid. The longer the payment is withholden, the better for you; for compound interest on compound interest is the rate and usage of this exchequer." The longer you put in extra efforts without being rewarded, the greater will be the quality and the quantity of your rewards when they finally come.

Everything that I've been discussing above repeats and reiterates the law of correspondence. Your outer world of results, of health and wealth and happiness, will always reflect your inner world of thoughts and emotions and preparation. Success is an 80–20 proposition, and 80 percent or more of your success will be determined by the quality of your thinking. This is why I have encouraged you to develop the habit of thoughtfulness, the habit of thinking carefully about who you are and where you're going, and especially of keeping your thoughts and words positive and constructive. Talk and think about what you want in life, and keep your thoughts and your words off of what you don't want. Talk about, think about, and work toward your major goals all the time.

In the final analysis, the key to positive, constructive living is goals, and all else is commentary. If you keep your goal as your vision of your ideal future before you, then every day you will continue to grow more surely toward the stars.

Major Points

- The critical factor in getting the use of other people's money is ROI, or return on investment.
- Successful people are motivated by inspiration, imagination, intelligence, and initiative.
- You are compensated in direct proportion to the value of your contribution.
- Management is getting results through others.
- Planning roots out flaws that can be extremely costly later.
- When you delegate a task, give authority commensurate with responsibility.
- The person who is getting paid to do the job is responsible for the work.
- The basic formula for management is *talent times relationships equals productivity*, or T x R = P.

Printed in the USA
CPSIA information can be obtained
at www.ICGtesting.com
JSHW010918040524
62494JS00004B/10

9 781722 506728